LEARN TO LEAD,
LEAD TO LEARN

LEARN TO LEAD, LEAD TO LEARN

Leadership as a Work in Progress

Mary B. Herrmann

Rowman & Littlefield
Lanham • Boulder • New York • London

Published by Rowman & Littlefield
A wholly owned subsidiary of The Rowman & Littlefield Publishing Group, Inc.
4501 Forbes Boulevard, Suite 200, Lanham, Maryland 20706
www.rowman.com

6 Tinworth Street, London SE11 5AL, United Kingdom

British Library Cataloguing in Publication Information Available

Library of Congress Control Number: 2019949316

ISBN: 978-1-4758-4148-0 (cloth)
ISBN: 978-1-4758-4149-7 (pbk.)
ISBN: 978-1-4758-4150-3 (electronic)

Contents

Preface

While enjoying lunch together in a beautiful quiet setting, a super-intendent colleague and I thoughtfully reflected on the essence of our work as leaders. We shared stories about our leadership careers in multiple districts. We discussed our aspirations, vulnerabilities, frustrations, failures, and successes. Above all, we talked about the journey—the constant learning, the incredible challenges, and the significant contributions.

Leading schools, like all leadership roles, is highly personal and complex. It is about constant learning in multiple dimensions simultaneously. There is the potential for both high risk and high impact. The leadership journey exists within a deep web of complexity and is fraught with a high degree of uncertainty. It is both exhilarating and terrifying.

Leadership is a work in progress. We hope that learning and experience contribute to greater effectiveness, but is this always the case? My colleague and I considered the question relative to our own leadership journeys. We agreed that when we started as leaders our learning curve was massive. We expected it to be and others accepted that. It was also complemented by an innocence or a sense of idealism that was not yet tainted. Did that idealism make us more effective or just more hopeful?

As leaders, we both grew to understand that our idealism pursued with innocence and passion as rookies took much greater courage and intentionality as experienced leaders.

The same was true with learning. Earlier in our careers, it felt like we were learning constantly, and our new learning was transformational. As our journeys progressed and we were expected to know more, our learning became less explicit and more uncomfortable. Once confident with how much we knew, we are now certain of how little we know.

Contributing Leaders

I am grateful to the incredible and inspiring leaders who shared their learning and leadership stories with me. Their anecdotal comments are embedded throughout the book. Their individual and collective experiences span multiple districts across the United States.

Dr. Ken Arndt—Ohio and Illinois

Dr. David Behlow—Wisconsin, Minnesota, and Illinois

Dr. Marsha Chappelow—Kansas and Missouri

Dr. Jennifer Cheatham—Illinois, California, and Wisconsin

Dr. Sarah Jerome—Wisconsin and Illinois

Dr. Kelley Kalinich—Georgia and Illinois

Dr. Keith Marty—Wisconsin and Missouri

Dr. Max McGee—Illinois, New Jersey, and California

Dr. Eric Witherspoon—Indiana, Iowa, and Illinois

Introduction

As leaders, we all recognize the importance of learning, but to what extent do we make learning central to our leadership? The position of an educational leader has become increasingly more complex. Many of the practices and habits that worked in the past are no longer sufficient or effective in this new learning economy.

Everything in our world today revolves around fast-paced learning. Leaders must embrace a world that uses knowledge to build more knowledge. Learning opportunities come from everywhere and leaders must be able to recognize this, share knowledge broadly, and use a wide array of networks extensively and successfully. They must be able to efficiently and thoughtfully problem solve, adapt, and innovate. It is the leader's capacity to learn and effectively apply learning that determines whether a leader can stay relevant and make an impact.

This book examines the factors that impact our ability and willingness to be shaped and transformed by our learning. To truly learn for impact, leaders need to grow the personal capacity to adapt and transform learning into action. Unfortunately, there are many factors that contribute to our lack of deep and dynamic learning. Most importantly, real learning is uncomfortable. In our fast-moving and success-driven culture, the intentional iterative processes and habitual practices that enhance learning are often not valued. Researchers have found, however, that across all sectors, effective, high-performing leaders who continually strive to "learn it all" outperform leaders who think they "know it all."[1]

This book is based on the assumption that learning is essential to our ability to adapt and innovate as individuals and organizations. For our schools and organizations to thrive, our leaders must be, first and foremost, voracious learners who create, nurture, and sustain conditions that enhance learning individually and collectively.

The purpose of this book is to help uncover some of the essential attributes and practices that are key to learning and leading. Eight leadership growth attributes are highlighted that, when developed and reinforced through iterative practice enhance learning and the capacity to adapt and transform. The leader attributes include *aspiration and agility; curiosity and intellectual humility; courage and rebelliousness; and enthusiasm and a driving spirit.*

The leader must also ensure that the organization is equipped to continually learn and grow. Related to each personal attribute, there is a similar organizational growth attribute that when effectively integrated can enhance organizational learning and the capacity of the organization to adapt and innovate. The eight organizational attributes include *purpose and imagination; exploration and diversity; organizational justice and disruption; and urgency and bold moves.*

Organization

The book is organized around the key attributes of personal and organizational growth. Section I includes chapters 1–5 and focuses on key attributes of personal growth. Section II includes chapters 6–10 and focuses on complementary organizational growth attributes that foster organizational learning. Chapter 10 brings it all together.

The book cites a wide array of research and embeds anecdotal insights from highly respected, district-level leaders (identified in the Preface) who generously reflected on their personal leadership journeys. Leaders were asked to consider the prompt—*Think about when you started your leadership journey and discuss in what ways you are a different leader today.* Readers are encouraged to do the same.

At the end of each chapter, there are related questions for further reflection. These questions incite readers to think about their own learning and how it can impact organizational learning, adaptation, and innovation. As Heifetz, Grashow, and Linsky[2] so eloquently state, "Adaptive Leadership is specifically about change that enables the capacity to thrive. New environments and new dreams demand new strategies and abilities, as well as the leadership to mobilize them."

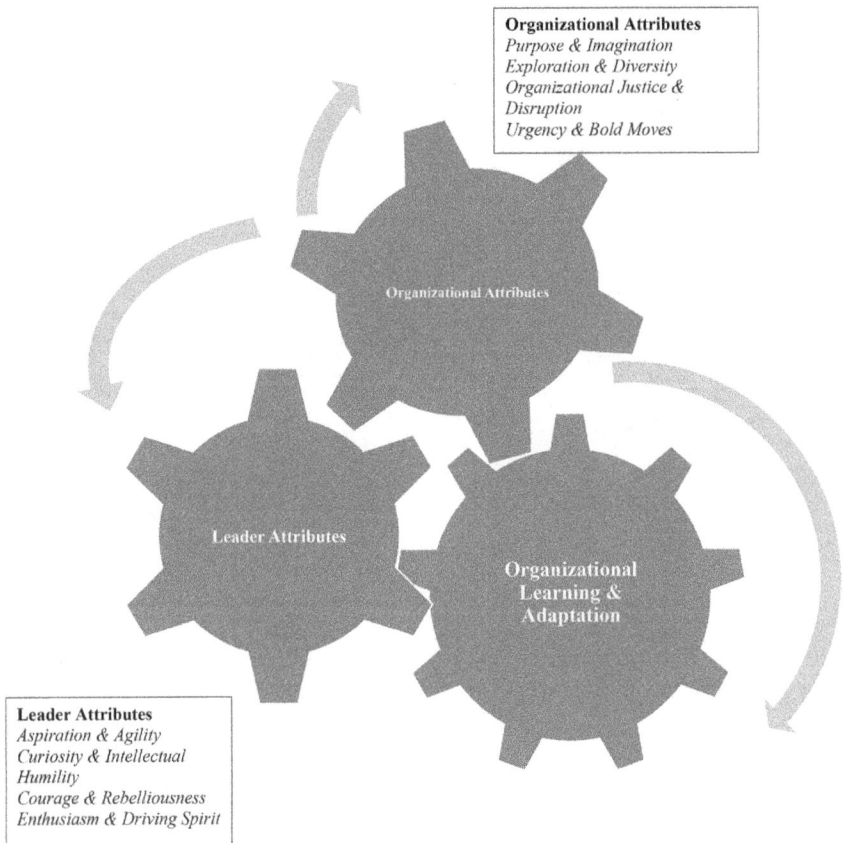

Organizational Attributes
Purpose & Imagination
Exploration & Diversity
Organizational Justice &
Disruption
Urgency & Bold Moves

Organizational Attributes

Leader Attributes

Organizational
Learning &
Adaptation

Leader Attributes
Aspiration & Agility
Curiosity & Intellectual
Humility
Courage & Rebelliousness
Enthusiasm & Driving Spirit

Figure 0.1.   Leader and Organizational Growth Attributes

Part I

LEADER GROWTH ATTRIBUTES

Chapter 1 addresses the significance of learning to lead. Learning is essential at both individual and organizational levels. Since so much of what we know about leadership development begins with a focus on self, it is understandable that the focus of the first section of the book is on building within each leader the capacity for deeper, personal learning.

In chapters 2–5, eight personal growth attributes that support and enhance personal learning and adaptation are addressed. These attributes have been identified through research and documented experiences across an array of disciplines and sectors. Each leadership growth attribute is essential to building one's capacity as a dynamic learner who can lead an organization that adapts, innovates, and makes a positive impact. The leader growth attributes include *aspiration and agility; curiosity and intellectual humility; courage and rebelliousness; and enthusiasm and a driving spirit.*

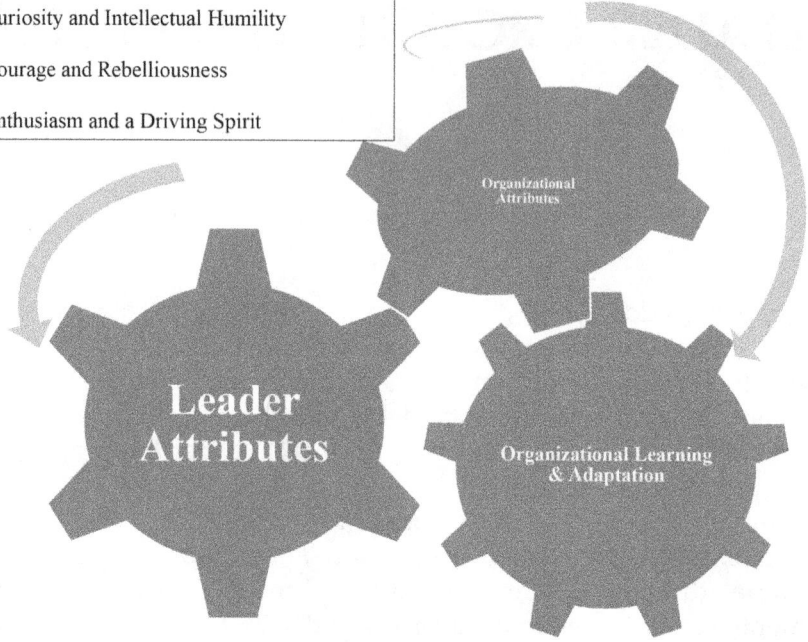

Leader Growth Attributes

Aspiration and Agility

Curiosity and Intellectual Humility

Courage and Rebelliousness

Enthusiasm and a Driving Spirit

Organizational Attributes

Leader Attributes

Organizational Learning & Adaptation

Figure S1.1.   Leader Growth Attributes

1

Learning to Lead

Leadership and learning are indispensable to each other.
—John F. Kennedy

There is nothing more significant to our leadership than our capacity to continually learn. In essence, our world is a laboratory for learning, and the context of our work is a new frontier. Margaret Wheatley[1] asks us to engage our *dwelling mind* as we remain open, patient, and humble; totally in awe of all we have to learn.

In this chapter, we will examine several factors and conditions that make learning and leading indispensable to each other, including the learning economy, the distinction between knowing and learning, learning agility, learning over the life span, and the forces that shape thinking and learning.

The Learning Economy

The nature and intensity of learning has changed over time as our world has grown increasingly complex. According to Bradley Staats, author of *Never Stop Learning*,[2] we are now living, working, and fully immersed in a "learning economy." Like all significant economic shifts, the dynamics of this learning economy impacts the way we absorb information, process it, and act as leaders. In order to thrive in this new economy, leaders in all sectors need to be mindful of and adapt to these new dynamics.

7

Staats describes the learning economy as characterized by four related dynamics or drivers: routinization, specialization, globalization, and individual scalability.[3] Routinization refers to the rapid growth of nonroutine jobs over routine ones. Nonroutine cognitive jobs have grown at a particularly fast rate, while both routine cognitive and routine manual jobs have slightly declined or remained relatively flat. In essence, the nature and schedule of work is changing. This has had a profound impact on how leaders define the scope of their work and how they manage and supervise their workforce. Even in PK–12 education, where the jobs remain stubbornly routine and the school schedule fairly predictable, there is growing desire for change and a rethinking of the school calendar, schedule, and routine nature of the work.

The second driver, specialization, refers to the growing number of specialists over generalists. For example, in 2017, the American Board of Medical Specialties recognized 37 specialties and 132 subspecialties—each requiring years of training.[4] Specialization requires an investment in the rapidly growing knowledge required to be effective and helps focus on the allocation of scarce resources. Unlike medicine, in the field of education, leaders are still following a more generalist model, where typically a small number of administrators are expected to learn and do it all.

The third driver is globalization. The work context today extends well beyond the local community with direct and indirect global connections. Even in the most remote communities, access to the world through technology influences the issues that impact what is learned and how.

Lastly, scalability refers to the ease in which we can now reach a much broader and diverse audience. Online learning and social media shape the nature of our work and our connections to others. Our professional networks are no longer limited to our local communities. We have the potential to connect with anyone, anywhere, at any time. These four drivers significantly impact the complex roles and responsibilities of leadership.

To thrive and make an impact in a learning economy, leaders need to be highly intentional and deeply invested in learning. They need to engage in deep iterative processes of continuous learning and the collective sharing and construction of new knowledge.

To this end, learning is a significant investment in time, energy, and attention. Given that leaders often feel overwhelmed in trying to address the wide array of expectations and constant demands of their constituencies, they often do not fully invest in their own personal learning. It is personal learning, however, that will ultimately help them the most in shaping their experiences and overall impact as a leader.

Even though they are committed to self-improvement, the reality is that when it comes to learning, leaders are often their own worst enemies. Instead of embracing behaviors and practices that enhance deep learning, leaders often engage in oppositional behaviors. For example, rather than learning from failure, they seek to avoid it at all costs. Leaders may also choose simple answers over probing questions and rush to solutions without clearly defining problems. Leaders typically view learning as a solo activity rather than a collective investment and resort to status quo practices rather than seeking novel ways of moving forward. Leaders often resist the struggle of deep learning, because learning is uncomfortable, frightening, and disruptive.

Knowing versus Learning

Most importantly, this new learning economy requires all workers and organizations to value learning over knowledge. The distinction between learning and knowing as a leader is profound.

This important distinction is well articulated by Tom Chi, entrepreneur, author, and speaker. As Chi describes, "When you're in knowing mode, it shuts down the capability of your brain to form new learning memories. When you're knowing you are trying to hold tight to your current sphere of knowledge. When you're learning, you are seeking to expand your sphere with new data and possibilities."[5]

We would like to think that we can both know and learn at the same time, but as Chi explains,[6] "It's hard to do any two verbs at the same time [think juggling and riding a bicycle]. It's even harder to be knowing and learning at the same time." And yet, we often conflate our experience of knowing and learning. There is tremendous tension between the two—we frequently mistake learning and knowing for each other—yet they are clearly distinct and have a significant impact on how we approach our leadership work.

Chi offers a framework to help leaders identify the knowing versus learning spheres. He asserts that as a leader it is essential to constantly be aware of which sphere you are operating in and to be able to reframe or switch your mode of operation. Chi[7] suggests the following simple exercise to help leaders shift from a knowing to a learning mode.

Start with yourself. Notice when you're in a knowing versus learning mode in conversations. Once you've developed an awareness, try shifting your stance from knowing to learning by asking yourself questions like "what else might be learned about this?" You might start to notice when others are in a knowing mode and engage them with questions to shift their mode to learning as well.

Learning Agility

Consistent with the argument that prioritizes learning over knowing, Heather McGowan, in her article "The Paradox of Education: Learning over Knowing,"[8] makes a compelling case for rethinking higher education as a destination, an earned degree that denotes "educated person," to a more purposeful objective of a person with learning agility, who is well equipped to adapt and apply new learning.

McGowan cites Deloitte University Press research that projects that by 2020, 50 percent of the content in an undergraduate degree will be obsolete in five years. This would suggest that the process of becoming educated is now likely longer than the shelf life of the knowledge, training, and degree that's gained.[9]

In order to continually adapt and thrive under rapidly changing conditions, leaders must forge and model a path forward that shifts the focus of organizational work and schooling from reinforcing "knowing" to prioritizing "learning." This cultural shift begins with the leader's commitment to continuous personal learning.

Learning across the Life Span

Our ability to fully engage in learning as leaders is impacted by a wide array of forces including personal aging and the way we process information. There is extensive research related to how we learn and how our capacity for learning evolves throughout our lifetimes. According to research from the National Academy of Sciences,[10]

> People continue to learn and grow throughout the life span, and their choices, motivation and capacity for self-regulation as well as their circumstances, influence how much and how well they learn and transfer their learning to new situations. People learn continually through active engagement across many settings within their environments; learning that occurs outside of compulsory educational environments is a function of the learner's motivation, interests and opportunities. Engagement with work (especially complex work that involves both intellectual and social demands), social engagement, physical exercise, and adequate sleep are all associated with life-long learning and healthy aging.[11]

The work of the educational leader is stimulating and complex. The old adage that *you can't teach an old dog new tricks* is not supported by research. Leaders have ample opportunities to continue to learn and grow, even as they grow older and become more seasoned in their roles. Leaders at all ages must recognize the potential for personal complacency and be intentional in motivating themselves to continue to learn.

Forces That Shape Our Thinking and Learning

In addition to research supporting the capacity for continuous growth in learning throughout one's life span, cognitive psychologists and neuroscientists have made tremendous gains in understanding the complexities associated with thinking and learning processes.

Most researchers concur that there are atleast two distinct modes of thinking processes. Daniel Kahneman,[12] winner of the Nobel prize in economics and author of *Thinking Fast and Slow*, labels these processes System 1 and System 2. Kahneman describes System 1 thinking as automatic, instinctive, and emotional. It relies on mental shortcuts that generate intuitive responses to problems as they arise. In contrast, System 2 thinking is slow, logical, and deliberate.

Each mode of thinking has distinct advantages and disadvantages. When we consider the implications for learning, System 1 allows us to take in information and reach conclusions efficiently and almost effortlessly by simply using intuition and rules of thumb. It enables us to respond quickly in a wide array of situations, but can also lead us astray in our decision-making. System 1 processing is particularly susceptible to bias and is more aligned with the knowing mode than the learning one.

System 2 processing in contrast is slower and more methodical. It takes considerable time and effort to continually ask probing questions, challenge assumptions, and engage in deeper levels of analysis. This mode of learning can ultimately lead to better decisions, but is often not conducive to the fast-paced, problem-solving expectations that are typical for educational leaders.

How can leaders foster an organizational environment that encourages System 2 thinking and learning over knowing? In the chapters that follow, we will discuss ways that leaders can enhance their own personal learning, as well as grow the capacity for learning in their organizations.

Questions for Further Reflection

1. In what ways have you personally and organizationally experienced and adapted to the new learning economy?

2. In considering the knowing and learning framework, in what mode do you typically operate?

3. In your district/organization, what would a shift from the perspective of "educated person" to a person who possesses "learning agility" look like?

4. To what extent do you engage in System 1 thinking over System 2? What can you do to increase more deliberate thinking and learning?

2

Aspiration and Agility

Becoming isn't about arriving somewhere or achieving a certain aim. I see it instead as forward motion, a means of evolving, a way to reach continuously toward a better life.

—Michelle Obama

Remember that first jolt? Your identity, your aspirations, and the leader you thought you were or aspired to be suddenly felt out of sync. People often envision a course for themselves that follows a fairly predictable path. But the realities of leadership are not at all predictable. Our first experiences with the messiness of leadership, the recognition that not everyone agrees with us or likes us or supports what we are doing—that the skills we once thought we had mastered do not work under different conditions—all shake our sense of who we are. Our identities are always evolving, and the leaders we aspire to be are a constant work in progress. Personal learning requires us to continually revisit who we are and to regularly address our contradictions. Essentially, learning brings us back to the role of novice again and again.

Aspiration

When we unpack the concept of identity and its relationship to the attributes of aspiration and agility, we begin to appreciate how central learning is to our leadership. How agile and resilient we are in pursuing our aspirations and the ways in which our personal mental model (identity) continues to evolve have a profound impact on our ability to continually learn and adapt.

Aspiration is an essential attribute for leaders. When we aspire to be an excellent leader (however we may define it), we strive in a long-lasting and meaningful way to achieve our aspirational identity. We envision a journey where we belong to an elite group of highly admired leaders whose values and behaviors are closely aligned, who seemingly effortlessly make excellent decisions, lead highly effective organizations, fulfill the organizational mission, and make an incredible difference in the world.

Even though our aspirations may be a catalyst for our leadership journey, the journey itself, however, is rarely aspirational and certainly not linear. We know that in reality, there are many curves, obstacles, and opportunities for derailment along the way. We have to be prepared for the possibility that sometimes, the journey follows a whole new path, wanders into unfamiliar territory, and shapes our identities in very different ways. Sometimes, what we learn and contribute along the way is very different from how we initially thought of ourselves and our most meaningful contributions, but ultimately shaping a new identity can be the greatest aspiration of all.

Identity and Labels

The personal mental model that we use to help us understand who we are—what we refer to as our identity—is complicated. It is shaped not only by what we hope or aspire to be, but all that we have been, as well. During the course of our lifetimes, we acquire a myriad of labels or descriptors that are shaped by both our personal characteristics, and how others interact and respond to us. These descriptors may include aspects of our life that we have no control over, such as where we were born or the color of our skin, as well as personal choices we've made in life, such as school district leader, spouse, parent, marathon runner, and the many other labels that describe something about ourselves.

Sometimes, these labels can be helpful and efficient in providing a shared sense of coherence and simplicity within a given culture or context. But simple labels (the baby is a boy or a girl) are also deeply embedded with bias and a wide array of hidden assumptions and expectations that can truly limit us. In our personal construction of our identity, the labels we have acquired over time, based in part by how others have perceived us, can restrict us in our capacity to express ourselves freely and openly.

Even though some of the labels related to our identity, like the color of our skin, may remain constant, the meaning we—and others—attach to these labels, and who we believe ourselves to be, is not fixed. Whether we recognize it or not, we are constantly changing and the same myriad of labels we use to describe ourselves need to evolve as well.

For example, early on in my leadership journey, I used the label of collaborator in describing the way I approached my work with others. Over time that label has taken on a deeper meaning and become more situational. Even though being collaborative is still an important part of my identity as a leader, I have also become more adept at being directive when necessary.

Narrative Identity

Our sense of identity is further constructed through the stories we tell ourselves about who we are.

> We are all storytellers—all engaged, as the anthropologist Mary Catherine Bateson puts it, in an "act of creation" of the "composition of our lives." Our identities and experiences are constantly shifting, and storytelling is how we make sense of it. By taking the disparate pieces of our lives and placing them together into a narrative, we create a unified whole that allows us to understand our lives as coherent—and coherence, psychologists say, is a key source of meaning.[1]

An important step in growing capacity to adapt as a leader is to regularly revisit and update one's "narrative identity." Northwestern University psychologist Dan McAdams describes narrative identity as an internalized story you create about yourself—your own personal myth.

> Like myths, our narrative identity contains heroes and villains that help us or hold us back, major events that determine the plot,

challenges overcome and suffering we have endured. This personal narrative plays an important role in shaping our thinking and behavior. . . . An individual's life story is not an exhaustive history of everything that has happened. Rather, we make what McAdams calls "narrative choices." Our stories tend to focus on the most extraordinary events, good and bad, because those are the experiences we need to make sense of and that shape us.[2]

Our narrative choices are significant. If we continue to tell ourselves the same story about who we are without updating it, we don't acknowledge how we have changed and continue to evolve as a result of our learning. When we fail to make our personal learning explicit, we have a tendency to feel more threatened by change. We are unable to recognize a change in ourselves, which makes it considerably more difficult to adapt to changing conditions.

Identity as a Leader

When it comes to our leadership, the relationship between the labels we use to express our identity and how we actually behave as a leader is complicated and can be tenuous, as well. Leadership is very personal and like other aspects of ourselves, it is an identity that we grow into. Many of us assume leadership roles and responsibilities throughout our lives, but the label of leader may not become part of our personal story until we identify it with a formal title (i.e., coordinator, director, principal, superintendent, board member, etc.).

The colleagues I interviewed reflected on their personal experiences identifying as a leader. David[3] talked about assuming a leadership role very early as a student teacher when he often found himself in pedagogical disagreements with his site supervisor. He learned to express himself in a respectful and politically sensible way, while still remaining true to his beliefs—this experience helped him to tactfully influence others as he assumed roles with more formal labels and authority.

Marsha[4] found that when she transitioned from the classroom to a formal leadership role, the values and skills that were important in the classroom, and an important part of her identity as a teacher, such as building relationships, listening and clearly communicating, planning and organizing, keeping the end in mind, having a sense of humor, and taking responsibility for one's actions, shifted in focus as an administrator. When she acquired the new label of administrator, she needed to adapt her skill set to better address adult behaviors and issues.

Since the labels we acquire throughout our lives have a cumulative effect, they can have tremendous implications for our identities as leaders. In essence, the process of becoming a leader can be tempered by the other identities we have assumed over time. Labels like woman, daughter, wife, mother, student, teacher, principal, superintendent, and so forth, all bring with them a set of assumptions and behavioral expectations that become a part of one's personal story.

Other less formalized descriptive labels like *bad at math* or *terrified public speaker* can also become a part of our how we see ourselves. Our identities, with all these different labels, can accentuate our strengths and our weaknesses. If we see these labels as permanent, or our identity as a whole as fixed, we unwittingly limit ourselves and our capacity to lead. This is especially true as Ibarra expresses, if our fixed labels "make it more difficult to step up as the situation demands something different."[5]

Jennifer[6] reports that the greatest impact on her identity as a leader was the recognition of what it means to be white and experience white privilege. Although her color itself may be a fixed aspect of her identity, how she constructed meaning related to the color of her skin changed dramatically over time through her intentional efforts to seek greater understanding. This recognition has defined her leadership mission and role in significant ways.

A leader's racial identity has a powerful impact on one's identity as a leader. The concept of white privilege (regardless of one's race) plays a significant role in how we see ourselves and others see us. According to consultant Francis Kendall, who specializes in issues of diversity and white privilege, "one's whiteness should be viewed as a built-in advantage, separate from one's level of income or effort. . . . White privilege means having greater access to power and resources than people of color [in the same situation] do."[7] Leaders who are people of color are very likely to experience barriers that their white counterparts don't.

Grappling with the meaning of one's racial identity is deeply complex and requires intentional effort. Similarly, one's perception of gender shapes one's identity in profound ways. Leaders who identify as females share a wide array of complicated experiences and expectations when trying to navigate executive roles that have been traditionally defined and dominated by males.

In addition to the labels that visibly differentiate us, there are those labels that are common to all of us. For example, social psychologist Dolly Chugh[8] argues that one important label we use to describe ourselves is "good person." Our moral and ethical identity is very important to us. Being a good person is a given, but like so many other aspects of our identity, we think of it as static or fixed, rather than something that is fluid and evolving.

Like all other labels we use to describe ourselves when we think of "good person" as a fixed part of our identity, it is harder to learn from our mistakes. We tend to explain them away when they don't fit within our definition of a good person. We may also excuse away behavior that we might question in someone else, because we are "good" and therefore our behavior must be acceptable, as well.

Our experiences as leaders continually shape our "sense of self," and like all other aspects of our identity, it is important to constantly revisit what it means to be a good and ethical person. When we are receptive to seeing our goodness along a growth continuum, rather than as a fixed asset, we are more receptive to becoming better people and more ethical leaders.

Identity Threats and Opportunities

The *good person* label, along with all of the other labels that contribute to our core sense of self, makes the part of our identity that calls us to lead especially complicated. Leadership is personal, emotional, and often visible. The very nature of leading requires us to try something new or different, and, in doing so, it often challenges aspects of our identity.

As we assume the role of leader, our behaviors may feel less authentic in relation to who we believe ourselves to be. For example, moving into a first leadership role is a big leap. The job is not just a perceived promotion to another level within the organization; it is a very different job. Although a background, or previous identity, as an excellent teacher can be extremely beneficial in terms of instructional expertise and credibility with teachers, the role of administrator is not the same as the role of teacher. Being an exemplary teacher does not translate into being an excellent administrator/leader. The same is true for a highly competent building level leader who assumes the role of a district-wide leader, only to be faced with the unique new challenges and compromises of being directly accountable to a board of education.

It is very humbling to move from seeing oneself as exemplary or exceptional to becoming a novice again. One's identity or sense of self changes and this happens repeatedly as one transitions into different roles or faces increasing levels of complexity within one's current position. As Sarah[9] so eloquently stated, "constant learning and change requires us to regularly revisit the novice role and begin again. There is vulnerability with every new situation and multiple compromises with oneself."

Agility

So how does one's sense of identity and accompanying narrative change or adapt to these new roles or complex situations?

Leaders find different ways to adapt and some ways are more agile than others. In the book *Act Like a Leader, Think Like a Leader*,[10] Ibarra describes the different practices leaders use to adapt to new situations. Although all leaders use multiple strategies, there are those who could best be described as *true-to-selfers*, who focus on one's core values and the comfortable and familiar "tried and true practices." These individuals may feel comfortable with their sense of authenticity, but struggle with trying to embrace a new and perhaps more effective way of behaving as the context changes. Perceiving their identities as being more fixed, *true-to-selfers* may find it more difficult to reconcile one's mental model and once-effective behaviors, with new expectations and demands in a rapidly changing political context. They may demonstrate agility by choosing to leave a position rather than accept, what they perceive to be the lack of authenticity and compromise required to thrive in their leadership role.

There are also those who tend to be more like "shape-shifters" (essentially chameleons), who easily adapt to the demands of a new situation with new and different ways of behaving. They have core selves defined by their values, but shift shapes depending on the situation. Ibarra cites David Remnick, biographer, in describing Obama's incredible political rise as one that required "extreme agility." "Obama worked hard to develop his broad stylistic repertory, he shifted accents and cadences depending on the audience: a more straight up delivery for a luncheon of business people in the loop (downtown Chicago); a folksier approach at a downstate V.F.W.; echoes of the pastors of the black church when he was in one." In essence, chameleons (shape-shifters) are comfortable adapting to the demands of a situation without feeling fake. They have no qualms about shifting shapes in pursuit of their convictions.[11]

Several of the leaders interviewed depicted their values as remaining steadfast, but described different ways of manifesting them throughout their leadership journeys. They also talked about the satisfaction that comes, often later in one's career, from knowing you can walk away from a leadership role if the compromises are too great. Keith described the joy of being in a position where he was not dependent on the position for his livelihood, but rather for the sense of efficacy he derived from the work. There is tremendous freedom in being able to confidently resist compromising one's values or sense of self, even if asked to do so.

Emotional Agility

Sarah[12] described the smaller compromises that you make with yourself as being a familiar part of the leadership journey. "There is a bargain that you accept when you enter a leadership position." She compares it to a young couple who while thinking about having children have a somewhat idealistic perspective of how they will parent. When they actually become parents, however, they experience the complexities associated with raising unique little human beings and find themselves regularly compromising on some of their ideals.

The same is true with district leaders; they can come to the position with lofty expectations and a certainty of thought about how to proceed, only to discover the many competing interests, beliefs, and expectations of the people they serve and the boards to whom they are accountable.

These relationships and the expectations laid out by the board to the leader can challenge one's identity in positive ways that can stretch and enhance learning, or in negative ways that can easily disappoint and disarm the leader.

Despite efforts to remain calm and measured, most leaders agree that leadership is emotional. Navigating the highly political nature of board relationships is in many ways unique and can be particularly draining. We accept the challenges of leadership because we are passionate about our mission and we know that leaders make a difference. How we accept and understand our emotions, however, can impact how adaptive and effective we are as leaders.

It is essential, therefore, to strive to accept and understand our emotions. When we are emotionally agile, we are able to identify and respond appropriately to our emotions. According to psychologist Susan David,

> The most agile, resilient individuals, teams, organizations, families, communities are built on an openness to the normal human emotions . . . our emotions contain flashing lights to things that we care about. We tend not to feel strong emotion to stuff that doesn't mean anything in our worlds. If you feel rage when you read the news, that rage is a signpost, perhaps, that you value equity and fairness—and an opportunity to take active steps to shape your life in that direction. When we are open to the difficult emotions, we are able to generate responses that are values-aligned.[13]

Reinvention

Our emotions can help us recognize if our identity as a leader becomes incongruent with who we believe we are or want to be, in essence our aspirational identity. If this happens, we may need to make a change. Sometimes, we need to rewrite our story. According to executive coach Monique Valcour, "Reconstituting our stories so that they help us move in the direction we want to go is a process of choice and intentional sensemaking."[14] Through this process of rethinking and rewriting our story, we may discover that the position we are in may no longer be a match or we may come to realize that what we can contribute is no longer of value to the organization or community. This is a critical discovery. As David reminds us, "you never want to stay in a district past your expiration date."[15]

Ken[16] talked about an experience in one district that drew a high degree of press coverage and national visibility. He recognized that even though there was support for his actions, he would always be defined by that event. If he wanted to rewrite his leadership story, it was important to move on.

This was a common sentiment, further reinforced by all the leaders interviewed. In each case, a new context elicited an opportunity to reinvent oneself and rewrite one's story to become better aligned with one's aspirational identity. When we close one chapter, we can start another. The greatest discovery is that we can manifest our aspirations and passion in many different ways.

Jennifer[17] characterized her professional journey as being somewhat of an "accidental routine," where she moved in and out of PreK–12 education and other nonprofit positions. The nonprofit work served as somewhat of a respite from the all-consuming work of district leadership, while at the same time inspired new learning and challenges. Each new position was an opportunity for revitalization.

David[18] described his own career as one of an "accidental superintendent." Because he was always a person who was willing to take risks, he was comfortable with stepping into new roles and did so when the opportunities presented themselves. Even within the same role, he often found himself transforming into someone else in order to meet the needs of the moment. As a personally described "introvert," he thought of much of his role as a performance. He considered board meetings and other large district community events as "showtime." In other words, he regarded his identity as being *momentarily fluid* and always evolving.

Momentarily fluid is a powerful way to think about identity. Not only are leaders adapting over time in significant ways, but they are also adapting their identities situationally. Even though David described himself with labels more aligned with being an introvert, when it came to "showtime" he was able to move outside his comfort zone and perform in a way that more easily connected with his audience.

When leaders are agile, they are flexible, resilient, and open to change and growth. They listen intently, learn continuously, navigate creatively, and respond quickly and fluidly. They are comfortable, and often thrive, with the constant discomfort, complexity, and messiness of leadership.

Questions for Further Reflection

1. What is your leadership story? How has it changed over time?

2. Consider a challenge or problem you are trying to solve—what is the story you've told yourself about the issue?

3. As a leader, do you tend to be more of a "true-to-selfer" or "shape-shifter"?

4. What is your story of reinvention?

3

Curiosity and Intellectual Humility

The important thing is not to stop questioning. Curiosity has its own reason for existence.

—Albert Einstein

We see it all the time with young children: constant and persistent questioning. Kids ask questions simply because they are curious. They want to better understand their world. They also persevere with their questioning so they can complete a task or project. Unlike adults, children interact with the world primarily through questions. In one study it was found that 70–80 percent of kids' dialogue consisted of questions, compared to a range of 15–25 percent for adults.[1] Curiosity is a powerful driving force for children and should be for adults, as well. It makes us try something until we can do it, or think about something until we understand it. It makes sense then, that curiosity is an essential attribute for leaders.

In this chapter, we discuss the curiosity, mind-set, and intellectual humility necessary for continuous learning and adaptation.

Curiosity

Adaptive leaders are voracious learners. In chapter 2, we discussed the significance of our personal identity and how, through our aspirational and agile behavior, it continues to evolve with our new learning. A natural enthusiasm and passion for learning is also key to continuous growth and adaptation. This enthusiasm is fueled by curiosity.

It is troubling, however, that we rarely use the descriptor, curious, when talking about district leaders. Curiosity suggests a strong desire to learn it all, not act as one knows it all. It is not that leaders aren't curious, they generally are. It is unfortunate, however, that in the public sector, leaders are reluctant to express curiosity freely, especially when addressing their constituents.

We have grown to expect, that in our highly politicized and often contentious environments, that leaders exude confidence and have the answers. When leaders don't, we attribute their lack of definitiveness to a sign of weakness, incompetence or indecisiveness. As leaders, we are often pressed to communicate succinctly and definitively. In doing so, we unwittingly accept the accountability to behave as experts, rather than pursue the opportunity to explore, experiment, and repeatedly play the role of avid learner.

Working with boards can be particularly challenging. The formalized board governance process does not easily accommodate uncertainty, exploration, or experimentation. Instead, leaders are expected to answer questions and provide direction. They typically prepare extensively for board meetings, ensuring that each member of the team is thoughtfully anticipating questions and prepared to answer them definitively.

The underlying assumption of board work is that answers are valued more than the inquiry itself and that "messiness" is to be avoided at all costs.

I currently serve as an elected trustee in my community. Serving in this capacity (especially as a former school superintendent) I appreciate the desire to have smooth running board meetings. They are far more desirable than meetings that are sabotaged by self-absorbed political agendas and negative discourse. I am grateful for the meticulous and extensive work of our administrative staff in preparing for tidy, well-orchestrated meetings, but I also struggle at times with the lack of opportunity to grapple together with the substance and messiness of complex inquiries. We are always mindful of long agendas and the perceptions of those who are watching. We rarely go deeper in challenging our assumptions and practices. This is often true at school board meetings, as well.

This focus on answers is not surprising, particularly with greater levels of complexity. Heifetz and Linsky observe that in complex times there becomes a "political marketplace for certainty and answers."[2]

Unfortunately, when the leader is an expert rather than a learner, an honest response of "I don't know" is rarely acceptable. Rather than reinforce the value of good questions that can lead to deep, informative inquiries, we often settle for easy, surface-level answers and quick fixes.

Our focus on answers more than questions narrows rather than broadens our world of possibilities. It also stifles our personal curiosity and natural inquisitiveness. Not only is curiosity essential to leadership and learning, but it has also been associated (in numerous studies) with better physical and mental health.[3]

Curiosity is central to learning and although some people may demonstrate it more visibly than others, all of us can continue to grow our sense of curiosity throughout our lifetimes. Curiosity is not a fixed attribute, but the mind-set we have relative to our learning plays a significant role in how we demonstrate it.

Mind-sets

In the Ted Talk, "Why You Think You're Right Even When You're Wrong," Julie Galef[4] suggests that in addition to the more cognitively based fixed and growth mind-sets popularized by Dweck there are distinct emotional mind-sets that represent profoundly different ways of approaching our learning and exploration.

Galef asserts that a good way to think about this relative to one's own identity is to begin with the question, "What do you most yearn for? Do you yearn to defend your own beliefs, or do you yearn to see the world as clearly as you can?" She contends that people respond to that question in ways that are consistent with a particular emotional mind-set. She further describes two distinct emotional mind-sets that she labels as *soldier and scout*.[5]

Galef argues that those who approach their exploration and problem-solving with a *soldier* mind-set are prone to defending their viewpoint at all costs. On the other hand, those who approach their exploration and inquiries as a *scout* are spurred primarily by curiosity.[6] This is consistent with the knowing versus learning framework discussed in chapter 1. What mode or mind-set are we using when we approach a problem or more broadly explore our world?

Beyond mind-set, we know from studies in neuroscience, that there are many cognitive biases, such as confirmation bias, and other hidden forces that impact our thinking and unwittingly impact our ability to explore freely. We also recognize that like most aspects of our identities, labels regarding our exploratory practices are fluid. The reality is that sometimes we behave more like a soldier than a scout, but growing our capacity to freely explore as a scout is worth our efforts. A dogged curiosity, in search of truth and understanding, is critical for leaders.

An adaptive leader constantly seeks truth and strives to understand reality. This cannot occur if one is constantly trying to defend one's own sense of *rightness*. There is considerable tension between one's pure desire to learn and one's desire to protect and defend one's identity. As we touched on in the first chapter, the label "good person" often interferes with one's deeper personal learning to become better.

The leaders I interviewed all agreed that the leadership journey is about constant exploration and discovery. Keith and Eric shared their perceptions that all of life is a classroom, waiting to be discovered by curious leaders. We are all students of leadership and opportunities to learn come from all sectors and walks of life. We must openly embrace these opportunities.

Intellectual Humility

In addition to being curious, leaders must be intellectually humble. It is easy to assume a higher level of confidence and expertise, as one becomes more experienced as a leader. Although there are valuable lessons that are learned through experience, these lessons can at times detract from new learning.

It is important for leaders to recognize that expertise itself is adaptive. In an interview on *Hidden Brain*, Harvard Business School professor Francesca Gino[7] describes how the infamous Captain Sully, who landed his plane in the Hudson River, defied what his previous preparation and training would have directed him to do—find the nearest airport—and instead opted for a totally unconventional plan.

Gino describes Captain Sully as someone with intellectual humility who rather than relying fully on his technical, in the box expertise, was able to problem solve by thinking outside the box. "He had that type of intellectual humility that kept him open-minded despite the fact that he had accumulated a lot of experience throughout his career."[8]

Keeping an open mind is essential for a leader. Our experiences are valuable, but they can't direct or define us. We must continue to evolve. My colleagues shared what they learned over time from their rich learning experiences and reflected on how their experiences helped inform the ways they approached new challenges. Their examples illustrate how one's experiences can further shape a growing and adaptive expertise, rather than a more fixed label of "expert."

Kelley[9] reflected on how through some difficult challenges, she grew a deeper understanding of the foundational work that needs to happen before a change occurs. She needed to let go of previous assumptions and grow her capacity to do the groundwork in clearly defining and articulating organizational goals. She learned to consistently approach her work from a systemic perspective.

Jennifer[10] shared that when she started her journey, she was very technical and strategic in her approach to leadership. She continues to use those skills, but over time has learned to lead with more humanity. She now pays more attention to the relationships and explicitly focuses on modeling for others what it means to lead with humanity.

Our experience and learning matters in our leadership, and despite our desire to avoid doing so, it is easy to fall into an "expertise" trap. Boards generally seek out leaders with experience and then, as mentioned previously, expect the leader to play the role of expert. Demonstrating what one knows while at the same time, humbly acknowledging all there is to learn, requires a high degree of finesse.

Finding a way to emphasize the power of learning over knowing is an ongoing challenge for leaders. Leaders receive both subtle and explicit messages from others related to expectations. For example,

I remember, when struggling with a situation, being reminded by those who I supervised that I was expected to know the answer, after all "that is why I was paid the big bucks."

Leaders are pressured to take on an expert role even when there are many downsides to doing so. There are countless examples from all sectors of how our training and so-called expertise can paralyze us from considering new possibilities. In fact, the more experienced we are the less likely we are to change our behavior.

Several of my colleagues shared this concern, as an impetus to take on new positions. It is scary to move out of one's comfort zone, but there is a certain freshness and vulnerability you encounter when you transition into a new position. There are countless opportunities for new learning when you are no longer bound by the expectations of the past. All were quick to clarify, however, that successful experiences in one district can inform your repertoire of behaviors, but do not directly translate into a successful application each time you move.

With each new experience, whether it is in an existing or new position, you enter the role of novice again. How effectively you embrace this novice role, is in the words of Michael Fullan, highly "nuanced." Fullan explains that "nuance leaders have a curiosity about what is possible, openness to other people, sensitivity to context, and a loyalty to a better future . . . (they are also) humble in the face of challenges, determined for the group to be successful and proud to celebrate success."[11]

Intellectual humility manifests itself in many ways. It is often demonstrated in our relationships, and in how we communicate with others. Trusting others and being trustworthy oneself is critical to being intellectually humble. Leaders demonstrate their humility by engaging others, throughout the organization and community, in learning as a collective endeavor. They also rely on colleagues and mentors to help them navigate their journeys. Demonstrating humility is in many ways a recognition of the belief that we are stronger together.

In many ways, humility is both an attribute and a behavior. Humble leaders recognize what they don't know, and also take responsibility for their actions. David shared that "humility is also about holding oneself accountable, not only for one's actions, but for one's ideas, as well."[12] Leaders must be able to accept the limitations of both their ideas and initiatives and be willing to adjust and/or change course when necessary.

Ken summarized the essence of intellectual humility by succinctly emphasizing the importance of being intentional about our learning. Over time he learned that the most powerful learning strategy he could model as a leader was to simply listen more. "We need to do more observing and listening than talking. In other words, leaders need to speak less and learn more."[13]

Questions for Further Reflection

1. In what ways has your curiosity impacted your leadership?

2. Would you describe yourself as having more of a soldier or scout mind-set? How would others describe you?

3. In what ways have you grown your adaptive expertise?

4. How do you demonstrate your intellectual humility?

4

Courage and Rebelliousness

Do one thing every day that scares you.

—Eleanor Roosevelt

The attributes we have discussed thus far (aspiration, agility, curiosity, and intellectual humility) all share two common threads: they can be continually developed and strengthened throughout one's lifetime, and they all enable meaningful learning and adaptation. The same is true for courage and rebelliousness. They are central to learning and leading. In this chapter, we will discuss the discomfort of leadership, fear of failure, courage, and the need for leaders to rebel.

Discomfort

Leadership is tough, demanding, frustrating, and uncomfortable. Leaders are expected to effectively navigate organizational complexity within a highly political context and make an impact. To do so requires tremendous courage and a commitment to something much greater than oneself. The decision to lead is a decision to act on one's values, and become vulnerable. Leaders who strive to make an impact cannot be bystanders in an inequitable and socially unjust world. Instead, they choose to give voice to those who have been unable to advocate for themselves. They choose to ask difficult questions and pursue agendas that are socially just and equitable, even when they are politically unpopular.

This does not mean that leaders do not experience fear. Leaders are constantly addressing fear in different ways—but they lean into the fear, rather than away from it. They choose to confront difficult situations rather than avoid them. This is significant.

To fully appreciate the discomfort of leadership, one needs to acknowledge the power of fear. Educational leaders must tolerate and embrace a high degree of ambiguity, uncertainty, and emotional exposure. This messiness makes leaders especially vulnerable and the act of leading particularly frightening.

In *Dare to Lead*, author Brené Brown states,

> You can do vulnerability or it can do you. Choosing to own our vulnerability and do it consciously means learning how to rumble with this emotion and understand how it drives our thinking and behavior so we can stay aligned with our values and live in our integrity. Pretending that we don't do vulnerability means letting fear drive our thinking and behavior without our input or even awareness, which almost always leads to acting out or shutting down.[1]

Jennifer talks about the constant discomfort associated with leadership. "When you put yourself out there and advocate for what you believe, you make yourself vulnerable. You take personal and professional risks, because ultimately leadership for equity is about making real change, not superficial change, for those who have been limited, or even harmed, by the system as it exists. It is about making tough decisions."[2]

The power of social media makes leadership increasingly more challenging because often the most meaningful actions a leader may take, are frequently the most controversial. A leader's Google search will often reflect the messiness of a tough decisions and the controversy of challenging the status quo. Every bold move a leader takes can be widely shared and commented on. These actions, which often address the most complex and contentious issues, can be easily reduced to sound bites, without context, painfully scrutinized and forever documented.

Fear

Fear is a natural part of leadership and our inability to recognize it can lead to highly dysfunctional and ineffective behaviors. As

David stated, "you learn quickly that an important part of effective leadership is to feel and acknowledge your hurt."[3]

In order to adapt and grow, leaders must continually recognize and confront their fears. Brubaker and Mobley, authors of "Don't Let Your Inner Fears Destroy Your Careers,"[4] suggest that the following four fears are of greatest concern to leaders in executive positions:

- Fear of being wrong (failure)

- Fear of missing out

- Fear of not being good enough

- Fear of being victimized or taken advantage of (superintendent as a scapegoat)

Each of these fears can play a significant role in how leaders perceive their world, think about their context and options, and ultimately behave. The fear of failure is perhaps the most significant in considering one's evolving identity as a leader. This fear, in particular, has tremendous implications for personal and organizational learning and the ability to adapt.

Learning from Failure

Failure is as much a part of leadership as success; yet despite our best efforts, we do not prepare ourselves well for learning from failure. Staats argues that our "focus on success as leaders leads both to a fear of failure and to an inability to see the failure that occurs around us." When we fail, something has gone wrong and "wrong is painful."[5]

The pain and hurt from failure can be personally experienced in many uncomfortable ways, including embarrassment, shame or anxiety. For district leaders, mistakes and failures are not only visible and talked about in the work setting, but often in the larger community, as well. When living in a fishbowl-like environment, the experience of failure can easily shake our confidence and unsettle our sense of self. It is, therefore, natural and reasonable for us to "fear failure" even if it is valuable and can help move us forward.

Failure feels uncomfortable, and the only way to avoid failure, and the threat to our identities, is to avoid taking risks.

This instinct for self-preservation isn't surprising, but it is counterproductive to learning. Bear Grylls, author of *How to Stay Alive: The Ultimate Survival Guide for Any Situation*, attributes his success in developing survival tactics to experimentation and learning from repeated failures. These failures, however, were not the result of reckless behavior. In each situation, he extensively prepared, played out different scenarios, performed his best, failed, and through detailed analysis learned from each failure. It was only through repeated failures that he was able to hone in on what works.[6]

As educational leaders, physical survival may not be at stake, but the implications of not moving forward and adapting new behaviors to new world conditions are highly consequential to the students and communities we serve.

Courage

Acknowledging and facing one's fears is critical to leading courageously.

In her book *Everyday Courage for School Leaders*, Cathy Lassiter defines everyday courage "as a willful intentional act; executed after mindful deliberation; involving objective substantial risk to the actor; primarily motivated to bring about a noble good or worthy purpose; despite perhaps, the presence of the emotion of fear."[7]

Building courage is not something that is dependent upon heroic circumstances, but rather a continually strong and deliberate effort to act bravely when facing challenges and injustice. Lassiter describes four different dimensions of courage that are essential for school leaders. The four dimensions include moral courage, intellectual courage, empathetic courage, and disciplined courage. She defines them as follows:

- "Moral courage is standing up and acting when injustices occur, human rights are violated, or when persons are treated unfairly.

- Intellectual courage refers to challenging old assumptions and understandings and acting on new learnings and insights gleaned from experience and/or educational research.

- Empathetic courage is acknowledging personal bias and intentionally moving away from it in order to vicariously experience the trials and triumphs of others.

- Disciplined courage is about remaining steadfast, strategic, and deliberate in the face of inevitable setbacks and failures, for the greater good."[8]

The leaders I interviewed talked about their leadership journeys, and through their stories, I found countless demonstrations of how they behaved courageously. The following examples highlight each dimension.

Jennifer described when she first came to confront and interrogate her own white privilege. It was through this experience that she became morally committed to being an advocate and ally for those who are less privileged. This deep commitment has shaped her personal and professional work. Acting as an advocate and ally has also required tremendous courage to "walk the talk" often under deeply contentious political conditions.

Eric shared how he challenged the assumptions and practices of curriculum tracking. Using extensive data and research, he provided a compelling narrative for change and strategically built a strong coalition to tackle the highly political challenge of "detracking" the high school.

Max expressed how his passion for opportunity and access has shaped his leadership journey. With each new leadership opportunity, his greatest consideration was how he could positively impact the lives of others. Beginning with an initial focus on serving students with special needs he continued to strengthen his deeper sense of empathy, by deeply engaging with and supporting children in need in both his personal and professional life.

Ken talked about strategically weighing the benefits of a new innovative practice with overwhelming demands for the allocation of energy and resources. In an effort to preserve the focus and resources of the organization, he made tough, disciplined decisions about what new initiatives to take on and what to let go.

Sometimes when there is great pressure to adopt the latest fad, the most courageous response is to say "no."

Rebelliousness

Leaders act courageously when they stay open-minded and are willing to go off script. In other words, leaders who make an impact, rebel. In the book *Rebel Talent: Why it Pays to Break the Rules at Work and in Life*, Francesca Gino asserts that "Rebels are not troublemakers. They're not outcasts. Rebels are people who break rules that should be broken. They break rules that hold them and others back, and their way of rule-breaking is constructive rather than destructive. It creates positive change."[9]

In chapter 3, we addressed the importance of curiosity and intellectual humility. We discussed the value of seeking the truth over our sense of "rightness." In the knowing versus learning framework, questions can be used as leverage to move into a learning mode, talk deeply about assumptions, and challenge the status quo. Good questions can lead to learning and change. They can also be threatening and regarded by some as "rocking the boat" or as rebellious behavior.

Moving forward requires a degree of breaking away from what is, and venturing into what is possible. In essence, leadership requires us to rebel against the constraints and inequities of the current system that are no longer acceptable or effective. This means that one often needs to break the rules in order to transform the culture and recreate the organization. This is very difficult to do, because conformity is a natural driving force in our personal lives, organizations, and communities.

Eric talks about how when he first came to his district the culture was very adult-centered. The norms and practices he witnessed were exclusionary and hierarchical. He strategically rebelled against the historical practices and worked to "overtly, consciously and assertively advocate for a culture of acceptance, belonging, valuing and equity."[10]

Leaders regularly engage in behaviors that challenge and disrupt the status quo, but it is never easy. It takes courage. The roles that we are expected to play as leaders are highly scripted and deeply entrenched in tradition. Members of the internal organization, as well as the broader community, expect us to behave in certain ways.

As Gino articulates, "Throughout our careers, we are taught to conform to the status quo, to the opinions and behaviors of others, and to information that supports our views. The pressure only grows as we climb the organizational ladder. By the time we reach high-level positions, conformity has been so hammered into us that we perpetuate it."[11]

School leaders have been taught to "serve" their communities. But when commonly defined as "to act as a servant," it becomes a somewhat more tenuous ideal. Conforming to the notion of service as a leader can mean struggling with tension and contradiction. In serving our communities, do we work to better reflect them, or to change them and make them better? Ideally, we can do both, but not without tension. How we grapple with this tension and ultimately decide to act will inevitably meet the expectations of some and fall short for others. We know that often what is expected by one constituency is resisted or rejected by another.

Ken described it this way, "Assume and accept that you and your efforts, will not be liked by everyone—the law of the thirds— a third will probably support you, a third won't care and will do whatever they want, and another third will more actively resist."[12]

The notion of conformity is further challenged through the lens of white privilege and power. School leaders assert that their need to rebel is often precipitated by a deep, unwavering commitment. Jennifer describes how her deep commitment to equity leadership plays out as a constant, adaptive challenge. When you are explicit, passionate, and persistent about your focus as a leader, "you are constantly tested by your constituencies. You put yourself out there and the expectations are very high."[13]

When leaders choose to not conform and act instead on their deep commitments for the organization and community, they can become catalysts for transformational change. Leaders also recognize that their non-conformity can take an emotional toll. Non-conformity can contribute to further isolation and loss of identity for the leader.

Kelley shared that through the messiness of transformational change, it is easy to become more guarded and isolated. "The status quo is powerful and any action that goes against it can cause the leader to further question one's sense of belongingness and the trustworthiness of one's relationships with others."[14]

As David described, leadership is about providing "hope." In order to do so and move forward, leaders need to resist the constraints of systems that no longer work. They need to break status quo practices that are unjust or ineffective. For schools to truly innovate and transform, school leaders need to act courageously. They need to rebel.

Questions for Further Reflection

1. Describe what makes you most uncomfortable as a leader.

2. What are your greatest fears?

3. In what ways have you acted courageously?

4. When is it appropriate and necessary for you to rebel?

5

Enthusiasm and a Driving Spirit

There is a certain enthusiasm in liberty, that makes human nature rise above itself, in acts of bravery and heroism.
—Alexander Hamilton

Complementing the attributes of aspiration, agility, curiosity, intellectual humility, courage, and rebelliousness are the fueling forces of enthusiasm and drive. Leaders learn out of a sense of adventure and a driving desire to better understand and impact their world. They seek new learning opportunities through challenges and change. They thrive in complex situations that are messy and ambiguous. In this chapter, we will discuss how leaders adapt and innovate by strengthening their enthusiasm, sense of adventure, resilience, patience, and commitment to self-improvement.

Enthusiasm and Adventure

Leaders model both an enthusiasm for the work and a driving spirit to make a difference. With leadership comes a tremendous sense of wonderment, there is excitement for learning and both an intellectual and emotional curiosity that is constantly energized.

While some in leadership roles may be comfortable with managing the status quo, the leaders I talked with were passionate about disrupting it. They were constantly seeking a better way. To this end, they consistently shared mission-driven, aspirational stories of striving to make a positive impact and change the world.

Leaders demonstrate their enthusiasm for their work in different ways—some are demonstrably and gregariously enthusiastic. Others display enthusiasm by simply being present to others, engaged and passionate about the work. When leaders model enthusiasm, others follow with their own energy and passion.

Eric shared, "I never coast. I carry my excitement to everyone in the organization—and remind myself, that even on the toughest day "this is what I want." He described his approach to his work as "revitalizing" leadership, seeing every experience, regardless of whether it is a success or a failure, as an opportunity to learn."[1]

As a self-proclaimed introvert, David reflected on the enthusiasm he brought to his work. "Much of the job is a performance. Even when it was most difficult to put on a positive face. I did. Leaders must always convey energy and enthusiasm for the work. In this sense, we are all performers and the show must go on."[2]

The importance of enthusiasm for the work cannot be understated, but as our leaders describe, enthusiasm for the work alone is not sufficient. These leaders coupled their enthusiasm for the work with an equally strong passion for learning and adventure. When asked about how she continued to learn, Jennifer indicated that "learning is a given, it is just part of who I am."[3]

Leaders who continually learn thrive on new challenges. They seek new adventures and delight in new experiences. Max shared that he always had a sense of adventure, a desire for trying novel things. This sense of adventure led him to explore a wide array of new positions in different parts of the county. It was not simply his sense of adventure, however, that drove his movement. He was always cognizant of a greater sense of purpose and the potential impact of his leadership on others. With each potential move, he considered, "How will this new adventure for me impact the lives of others?"[4]

Resilience

Adventurous leaders and organizations also have the ability to bounce back when things don't go as planned. Resilience plays a prominent role in organizational learning. A leader's ability to bounce back from disappointment and failure is paramount to leading the organization forward. Extensive research suggests that leaders who demonstrate resiliency are more respected and effective. When Folkman analyzed self and direct report assessment data on 500 leaders, he found that when looking at the ratings of overall leadership effectiveness, it was clear that the most resilient leaders were viewed as the most effective leaders, as well.[5]

Effective leaders model, even under the most challenging circumstances, the ability to accept failure, learn from it, stay strong, and focus on the mission.

Even though resilient leaders and organizations may struggle under challenging circumstances, the struggles often lead to deeper learning and new strategies to persist in the important work that needs to be done. Leadership consultant Jesse Sostrin suggests that in many ways, resilience is a personal act of defiance. A moment of resilience is your chance to face adversity and say: "No, not today. You will not stop my momentum or reduce my potential to make the most of this opportunity."[6]

Patience

In these highly politicized and challenging positions, leaders can exude enthusiasm and learn to be more resilient, yet they still may experience a sense of restlessness. It is difficult to be patient. Working with a board is often challenging. As board members change, new relationships and dynamics come into play and district leaders often find themselves taking two steps backward to move one step forward. Trying to lead meaningful change, while navigating complicated relationships with board members, an array of political agendas with community members and working conditions-related issues with teacher unions can be frustrating.

Several leaders commented on how these factors impacted their patience, personal resilience, and learning. Sarah stated,

> This is complex work with multiple constituencies. It almost always requires the delicacy of compromise. There is a different kind of wisdom when you are immersed in the process of change—we have a deeper understanding of the complexity of the work and sometimes the compromises are too deep—I think

there is some point when you can no longer do it. Sometimes the patience just runs out in us.[7]

Sometimes, leaders seek new positions because they thrive on new adventures; other times, it may be more related to frustration, a bad match, or an inability to move forward quickly enough. Regardless, leaders should always consider the experience as an opportunity to learn.

Ken shared that he became a better administrator because he ventured outside his comfort zone and sought districts with different demographics. Keith found that a change of scenery truly re-energized him. Jennifer noted that her "accidental routine" of moving in and out of Pre-K education and other nonprofit work provided great opportunities to learn and contribute in different ways.

Self-Improvement

Another significant aspect of growing our capacity for learning is untapping the insatiable drive within us. So much of our learning as leaders is focused on improving the core work of the organization. In a highly content rich profession, we are constantly striving to integrate learning about new strategies, programs, and mandates. In many ways, the role of an educational leader is often perceived as an extension of the role of teacher with a relatively narrow lens of focus. The problem is that the district leader's role is far broader and more diffused.

District leaders are expected to understand instruction, curriculum, finance, personnel, facilities, organizational planning, governance, program evaluation, community engagement, and so on. The amount of information and content district administrators are expected to absorb and integrate is phenomenal. In a political culture where knowing is typically perceived more favorably than learning, absorbing content becomes a priority.

Leaders have little time to plan and focus on their own professional learning and growth. So how do leaders continue to learn and improve?

There are many pathways for continuous learning and improvement. In addition to learning from each leadership success and failure, the following are some more differentiated and formalized experiences our leaders shared.

Keith talked about the significant role, mentors and a strong network of colleagues have had in shaping his learning and leadership. He relies on trusted colleagues to help process meaning and problem-solve. He also reads extensively about leadership and has learned a lot from his study of military leaders. He values a cross-disciplinary approach to the study of leadership.[8]

Ken talked about the value of podcasts, blogs, and other digital media that address a wide array of topics, perspectives, and different approaches to problem-solving. He can tune in when it is convenient to do so and make personal connections as he engages with the content. He also finds value in professional organizations and quality conferences where he can network and learn from others.

Central to her learning, Jennifer indicated that her formal annual review is a great complement to her ongoing and iterative practices of self-reflection and feedback. Through these habitual processes, she identifies things that she wants to do better and redefines them as commitments that she shares with her team members, who in turn support her in her growth efforts.

District leaders frequently have a feedback-loop component as part of their evaluation process which can be very helpful in informing their improvement efforts. Others see things in us that we don't see, and their feedback can be invaluable. This is especially true when the process is perceived by all involved as trustworthy and credible. When others are asked to evaluate our effectiveness anonymously, however, often without a clear understanding of our position or responsibilities, it can feel insufficient and sometimes hurtful.

Sometimes, leaders may perceive a very formalized process that is connected to an evaluation, as being too leading or prescriptive. They may prefer a less formal way to solicit feedback from others. Leadership consultant and author Marc Effron describes an approach called "feedforward." With this approach, you ask a few people you trust how you can be a higher performer in the future. "This isn't feedback about the past, but a suggestion for what I should start, stop or continue to do to be a higher performer."[9] Engaging in a "feedforward" approach can enable more immediate adjustments and allow leaders to adapt quickly.

Life as a leader is fast-paced, messy, and complex. When leaders are intentional and highly committed to their own personal growth and self-improvement they can better adapt to their constantly changing conditions.

In most cases, however, leaders find that being intentional is not enough. Too often the allocation of time and the cultural conditions and expectations do not foster an environment conducive to dynamic learning.

In the next section, we will address the organizational conditions that support learning for all.

Questions for Further Reflection

1. In what ways do you demonstrate your enthusiasm for your work and personal learning?

2. What role does adventure play in your life as a leader?

3. How do you address the personal restlessness and impatience of your leadership struggles?

4. How do you continue to learn and improve?

Part II

ORGANIZATIONAL GROWTH ATTRIBUTES

In section I, we examined the personal leader growth attributes that enhance learning for impact. These attributes included *aspiration and agility; curiosity and intellectual humility; courage and rebelliousness; enthusiasm and a driving spirit*. In section II, we extend our focus to the organization. In order to build capacity and significantly embed learning for impact within the organizational culture, the leader intentionally and thoughtfully focuses not only on his/her own personal learning and growth, but also on the attributes that foster and enhance organizational learning, as well.

These attributes have been identified through research and documented experiences across an array of disciplines and sectors. In chapters 6–9, eight organizational growth attributes that support and enhance organizational learning and adaptation are addressed. Each of these attributes is a significant part of the deep and strategic leadership work that is focused on shaping and transforming the organizational culture. The organizational learning attributes include *purpose and imagination; exploration and diversity; organizational justice and disruption; and urgency and bold moves*.

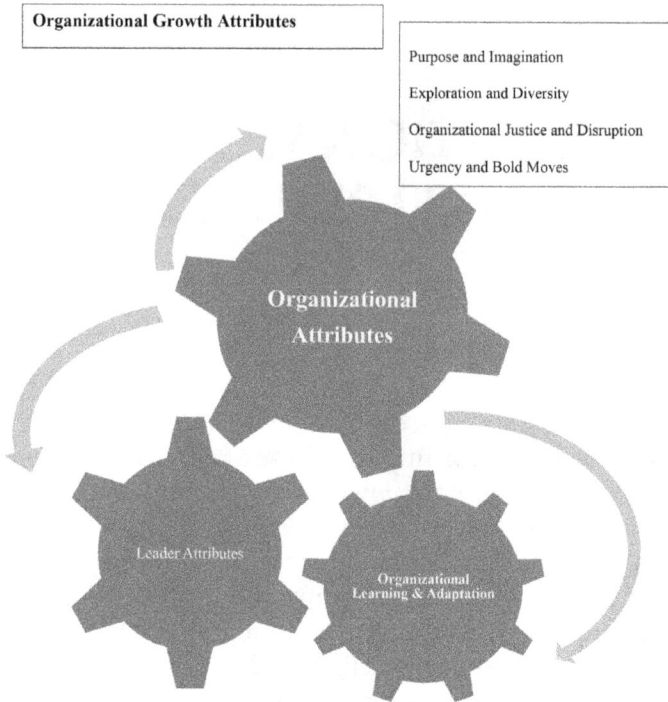

Organizational Growth Attributes

Purpose and Imagination

Exploration and Diversity

Organizational Justice and Disruption

Urgency and Bold Moves

Organizational Attributes

Leader Attributes

Organizational Learning & Adaptation

Figure S2.1.   Organizational Growth Attributes

6

Purpose and Imagination

The visionary starts with a clean sheet of paper, and re-imagines the world.

—Malcolm Gladwell

In chapter 2, we talked about the significance of one's personal identity and the fluid nature of how we evolve and rewrite our personal narratives. In our ongoing quest for coherence, our personal stories that tell us who we are can be played out as routine like scripts that are difficult to change. Learning is constantly filtered through these labels and stories, and it shapes what we do. To reinvent ourselves we must reconstruct our stories to adapt to our changing conditions and new learning. The same is true for our organizations. The aspirations we hold for our organizations evolve over time and are also a part of our leadership story.

In this chapter, we will discuss the stories we believe about our organizations, the role of the leader in shaping and rewriting the organizational narrative, and the need to reimagine our organizational identity and purpose.

Stories

Stories can be powerful sources of data about an organization. As a new leader, one is often overwhelmed by the stories that members are anxious and excited to share. Board members, teachers, parents, union representatives, and so on act quickly to gain access to the new leader's calendar to share their unique perspectives.

They share stories that reveal a lot of information about how the organization sees and values itself and how they may personally feel aligned or sidelined.

In organizations, the stories we tell ourselves truly matter. Our shared narratives can function as guiding principles or control mechanisms that communicate to all members of the organization what to value and how to behave. For example, one district described itself repeatedly as "unique and exceptional." This district narrative, widely shared, created a sense of pride in the district. Over time, however, it also helped foster a closed culture where there was little desire to learn from or network with others who were perceived as less exceptional. Opportunities for improvement were primarily technical in nature and did little to question assumptions or in any way disrupt the status quo. A significant leadership challenge, therefore, was to uncover the story and rewrite it to focus less on organizational greatness as a fixed entity and more on the greatness of organizational learning.

Through story shaping and sharing, leaders can craft powerful narratives that foster a sense of purpose. They can also communicate a passion for both personal and organizational learning. Essentially, leaders can take important data and turn them into stories.

Max[1] used storytelling extensively in his work as state superintendent in Illinois. When he provided a forum for people to share their personal stories regarding the consequences or potential impact of legislation, he gave voice to policy work. Stories touch both our hearts and our minds. They remind us of our purpose and help strengthen our sense of empathy and compassion. They bring a variety of personal perspectives to our work and deeply connect us to the people we serve.

As a district leader, I shadowed students and facilitated regular student advisory and focus groups. These experiences were powerful reminders of the incredible responsibility we have to serve all students well. My learning and the stories shaped by these experiences helped inform my decision-making and our focus as a school district. Originally, the stories were simple snapshots bound by place and time, but they evolved and gained meaning over time as we integrated them into a more comprehensive story of "us."

The student voice has now become an essential part of the larger narrative and continues to evolve as it captures new snapshots and stories.

Integration

It is essential that leaders integrate many different and diverse narratives, and never rely on a single story. In her TED Talk, the "Danger of a Single Story," novelist Chimamanda Adichie tells the story of how she found her authentic cultural voice and warns that if we hear only a single story about another person or country, we risk a critical misunderstanding.[2] As leaders, we have the responsibility to be open to and to actively seek to understand the many different stories and unique identities that shape our communities.

The leader plays an essential role in bringing diverse and often competing stories together to craft and articulate an identity for an organization. This is not a simple or single action taken by the leader, but rather an ongoing and fluid process of integration. According to Fullan (citing Mary Parker Follett), "leadership is fluid because it is always a process: Legitimate authority flows from coordination, not coordination from authority."[3]

The process of imagining an organization that honors and reflects the uniquely rich and diverse stories of its members while concurrently pushing them to pursue higher aspirations for the greater good requires a highly dedicated and intentional leadership focus.

Researcher and author Margaret Wheatley draws on experiences from social movements to help discern the role of the leader in articulating a sense of purpose. "Self-organizing requires a clear sense of identity known to everyone in the organization and the personal autonomy to figure out how to put that identity into action moment by moment. There will always be differences over which actions to pursue and that's as it should be. What's clear is that the identity is clearly visible in every action."[4]

She further explains that the role of the leader is to keep watch over the identity. "It is foolish to think it won't change as people make their own decisions regarding their actions. . . . If you lose focus and get absorbed in crises, you end up far from where you intended to be—more controlling, more bureaucratic, less trusting, more demanding, exhausted and wondering what happened."[5]

Wheatley reminds us that the role of the leader is significant. There is also a high degree of ambiguity and tension as the leader works to find a balance between providing too much direction and not enough. To be fully integrated the organizational identity must be clearly understood and shared by all.

Imagination

How we define "us" is critical to our work together. We construct (ideally together) the stories and labels that shape our identities as organizations, and in turn, our collective understanding of our identity defines our norms and practices. Like our personal identity, our organizational identity is not fixed. We can recreate and update our organizational narrative as our conditions change. In schools, there is a unique opportunity for reinvention with each new class of students, yet typically there is little change from one graduating class to another. While other organizations seek to redefine and reinvent themselves to address fast-paced rapidly changing conditions, schools remain remarkably the same.

In an NPR Freakonomics segment[6] focused on organizational change in our learning economy, the narrator describes how Ford Motor Company is reinventing itself to serve a broader purpose. The company is redefining the purpose and nature of its work to reflect changing needs and expectations by transforming from work that was originally defined as vehicle production to work that is now focused on the broader transportation service industry. It is no longer just about producing and selling cars; it is now about identifying and serving the basic transportation needs of its customers through a wide array of potential services including ride-sharing.

Many of the purposes that schools once served have changed, as well. Content knowledge and resources are no longer reserved for dissemination through schooling. For much of our population, there is now twenty-four hours, seven days a week access to unlimited information. The purpose of providing equal access and opportunities for all students has fallen short, as well. Inequities and injustices in education continue to persist. Most agree that the old stories that support traditional models of schooling are no longer sufficient. The identities of our educational institutions, much like our own, require a reinvention that adapts to new conditions and new learning.

In the book *Nuance*, Michael Fullan states that,

> Educational Entrepreneur and philanthropist, Ted Dintersmith finds that most education systems in the United States are working diligently "doing (obsolete) things better:" tests upon tests, learning experiences that have little meaning for the student, punitive evaluation, excruciating remedial work, and the like. In the meantime, the gap between high and low performers widens and even those who do well on tests are not prepared for life. The world is becoming more demanding at the very time that regular schooling is standing still.[7]

For leaders, both the challenges and opportunities are tremendous. Extensive deep learning over time increases the potential to imagine and construct new stories together, but it is never easy. As Sarah described, "getting a diverse group of people with unique stories and personal agendas to a shared sense of purpose is like learning to dance together."[8] There are many missteps and awkward moments, but when it happens there is a great sense of shared accomplishment and joy.

Keith[9] describes his personal leadership journey in embracing a deeper purpose. He describes how in his earlier years as a leader he committed to the concept of "all," but never fully appreciated what it meant. It wasn't until he started work in his current district that he and his team became more deeply invested in the reality of "serving all students." It has become the driving force of his leadership. This strong, shared sense of purpose is a powerful driver of change that connects and aligns all aspects of his organization. The district's renewed purpose informs all decisions and actions and comes with a no-excuses commitment—"all means all."

Leaders recognize that the power of change comes from identifying the narrative for the organization, and as a collective group, consciously choosing to live it. This iterative, non-linear process of thinking deeper about the purpose and who we want to be seeks to integrate our strongest aspirations. Regardless of the strategy or model used, the process is highly informed by our stories, present realities, and future scenarios. It is easy to become overly confident in the use of data and prescriptive processes, to find meaning and define purpose. In reality, the use of data and other strategic processes inform but do not replace the imagination and creativity of people coming together to envision something greater. A significant part of the role of the leader is to unleash the creativity and power of people to imagine and create a better world.

Questions for Further Reflection

1. What are the stories that shape the identity of your organization?

2. In what ways do you incorporate storytelling in your leadership practices?

3. How have you re-imagined your purpose as an organization?

4. How would other members of your organization/community describe your purpose?

7

Exploration and Diversity

When a leader approaches the process of leadership as continuous exploration, the organization becomes a frontier to be discovered. This is a fluid process that redefines the relationships and expectations of the leader within the context of the organization.
—Ronald Heifetz & Marty Linsky

Curious leaders who are intellectually humble inspire curious and creative organizations. In this chapter, we will focus on the leader's role in enhancing the organizational attributes of exploration and diversity to ensure organizational learning and adaptation. Specifically, we will discuss how leaders use inquiry, build capacity, and embrace diversity.

Lead through Inquiry

David shared that asking questions was central to his leadership. When we lead through inquiry, "we don't assume, we don't accept surface level responses, we keep asking why."[1]

Ken shared that he started every executive team meeting with the question, "What do we need to talk about?"[2] Rather than assuming that he owned the agenda, he would always ask his leadership team for their perspectives on what was important and what they needed to collectively grapple with.

As we discussed in chapter 3, good questions can be powerful tools to foster and shape our personal learning. Questions are valuable in ensuring that organizations continue to learn, as well. If an organization moves in the direction of its focus of study, then the leader through thoughtful questioning begins the process of transformation. When we are open to exploration and lead through intentional inquiry, we work to ensure that not only our people, but our organizations, as well, will continually learn and adapt.

The principles of appreciative inquiry[3] offer a conceptual frame work for thinking about the significant role of inquiry in organizational learning and change. The following information can be found on the AI website (table 7.1).[4]

These principles provide a powerful framework and rationale for recognizing the value of curious and thoughtful leadership. An organization that embraces inquiry and learning as a way of life will be better equipped to adapt and reinvent itself when addressing the complexities of changing conditions.

Table 7.1. Core Principles of Appreciative Inquiry

Principle	Summary	Details
• Constructionist principle	Words create worlds	Reality, as we know it, is a subjective versus objective state and is socially created through language and conversations.
• Simultaneity principle	Inquiry creates change	The moment we ask a question, we begin to create a change. "The questions we ask are fateful."
• Poetic principle	We can choose what we study	Teams and organizations, like open books, are endless sources of study and learning. What we choose to study makes a difference. It describes—even creates—the world as we know it.
• Anticipatory principle	Images inspire action	Human systems move in the direction of their images of the future. The more positive and hopeful the image of the future, the more positive the present-day action.
• Positive principle	Positive questions lead to positive change	Momentum for [small or] large-scale change requires large amounts of positive affect and social bonding. This momentum is best generated through positive questions that amplify the positive core.

Source: David L. Cooperrider and Diana Whitney, *A Positive Revolution in Change: Appreciative Inquiry* (Taos, NM: Corporation for Positive Change, 1999). https://appreciativeinquiry.champlain.edu/learn/appreciative-inquiry-introduction/5-classic-principles-ai/.

Leaders can use exploratory practices as a way to build on organizational strengths as in the appreciative inquiry approach. They can also use inquiry to disrupt the status quo and stimulate innovation. Business executive and author, Beth Comstock refers to this as "agitated inquiry." Through questioning the leader may seek out tension, because, as she states, "Innovation is not about reassurance or consensus; in fact, it often encourages confrontation."[5]

Build Capacity

Building capacity is a core responsibility of the leader. A humble leader recognizes that fulfilling one's vision and adapting to changing conditions is only possible when all members are deeply invested in the vision and engaged in doing the work that needs to be done. In learning communities, the contributions of all members are valued and new learning is constantly being integrated into the fabric of the culture.

New learning is often associated with professional development, but unfortunately many of the traditional approaches to professional development for educators are ineffective and inconsistent with what we know about how people learn.[6] Professional development is too often characterized as a day, or conference, or other activity rather than an ongoing systemic process for learning that is deeply embedded within the culture of the organization.

Stephanie Hirsh from *Learning Forward*[7] shares that there are many elements essential to establishing effective systems of professional learning. She highlights four cornerstones that she believes are critical to achieving the ambitious outcomes we all desire for students. These cornerstones to professional learning are built on and extend beyond the professional learning standards generated in 2011. The cornerstones include: lead with equity, invest in team learning, leverage high-quality instructional materials, and advocate with evidence.

These cornerstones are consistent with current research that emphasizes the significance of the group as the foundation of success in learning organizations. Fullan stresses the importance of developing unity of purpose and action with those in the organization and pursuing and staying the course through continuous interaction. The goal of "being right at the end of the meeting is a function of what he calls joint determination—the dynamic duo of leaders and followers working together and being open to one another's ideas."[8]

The lasting power of a group experience where all members are deeply engaged and equally invested can be transformational. The experience of learning and problem-solving together can have a lasting impact on the members of the group regardless of the organizational outcome.

As an assistant superintendent, I worked with a group of teachers and administrators to design an innovative new lab school as part of a solution to an overcrowded high school campus. Although our proposal was not ultimately selected as the best solution to the overcrowding, our collective inquiry provided a hopeful new vision for schooling that energized and transformed us professionally. At the same time, the fruits of our learning provided our district with new ways to think about our work.

David speaks of a similar intense, long term initiative as an assistant superintendent that remains one of the most memorable professional experiences of his career. Our conversation led us to question whether in the role of superintendent, it is possible to feel the high-intensity learning and passion that we both experienced in assistant superintendent roles. Unfortunately, the superintendent position, especially in larger districts, is often not a part of the deeper collective learning and struggles that can ultimately feel transformational to participants.

This discovery of not feeling as deeply connected to the work was shared by some colleagues as part of the loss that accompanied a change in position. Despite a potential lack of personal engagement in a process, it is essential that the district leader learn from, recognize, and honor the personal growth and investment of other participants.

Empower Others

Regardless of the context, deep learning experiences are only possible when leaders choose to empower others. One way to build capacity and share power is to delegate. In the article "To Be a Great Leader You Have to Learn to Delegate Well," the author describes the importance of thoughtful delegation by arguing that,

The upper limit of what's possible will increase only with each collaborator you empower to contribute their best work to your shared priorities. Likewise, your power decreases with every initiative you unnecessarily hang on to. While it may seem difficult, elevating your impact requires you to embrace an unavoidable leadership paradox: you need to be more essential and less involved.[9]

Empowering others and delegating effectively requires a willingness to let go of the work and to trust others. It is difficult to do when the leader is held accountable for the work, regardless of who completes it. When empowering others the leader must be intentional about expectations, but also willing to accept and learn from mistakes.

The leader must also be cognizant of the most efficient and effective ways to meaningfully collaborate and empower others in the work. Frequently, educational leaders work under the assumption that if we just bring people together, they will collaborate effectively and work productively. We have a wide array of committees and teams that meet regularly in our schools. We rarely, however, assess whether our coming together truly enhances our learning, relationships, and work productivity.

When considering the value of coming together, an important part of the equation must be the time and money expended. Boudett and City in their book *Meeting Wise* offer a formula to estimate the annual (financial) investment in a meeting. Essentially, you "multiply the number of people at the meeting by the number of hours in the meetings by the average hourly earnings of the people in the meeting by the number of meetings per year."[10]

This reminds us that when we bring people together, and truly empower others in meaningful ways, we must be purposeful and intentional in what we plan to accomplish and well prepared to ensure growth-oriented and productive outcomes.

Delegate

Successful delegation to individuals or teams requires a relationship based on trust and deliberate action that sets up the conditions for success. A leader cannot simply hand over a task to another individual or team and expect meaningful learning and productivity.

When leaders strive to build capacity through delegation, they work to ensure that the following conditions are in place: The assigned work is meaningful and purposeful; the work is aligned with the greater goals and mission of the organization; and the individuals or team assigned have (or will receive) the knowledge and training needed to be successful in carrying out the work. Furthermore, the leader is abundantly clear about the expectations for growth and quality work and explicit about the individual or group's authority, responsibilities, and decision-making potential.

Empowering individuals and teams in meaningful work contributes to a greater sense of efficacy and ultimately builds capacity within the organization. This capacity is always dependent on both individual and organizational learning. To this end, Fullan describes the nuanced role of the leader. "Leaders learn and lead in equal measure. They help scores of others do the same. This is the deep meaning of learning systems. They are stocked with people who see learning as the norm, who know that you can't lead without learning, and who seek breakthroughs by mobilizing these capacities in others."[11]

Embrace Diversity

In the *Hidden Brain* podcast entitled "The Edge Effect," Shankar Vedantam highlights research that supports the contention that there is a strong connection between diversity and creativity. He features one study by Harvard economist Richard Freeman that found that most scientists in the United States seem to stick with their own kind when working together on a project. When scientists branched out to collaborate with colleagues from different backgrounds, however, their publications were more likely to receive more citations and greater recognition. "Psychology research out of Tufts University has found something similar. When you introduce racial diversity into a group, all the people in the group begin to broaden the scope of their thinking and explore more options."[12]

This is not surprising. If the circle of connections is too tight and the members of it too similar, it is easy to become trapped in an echo chamber where the same ideas keep circulating. The so-called echo chamber in school life is especially problematic and all too common. It is easy to become insulated and isolated.

Educators often feel the burden of increased public scrutiny and accountability, and when feeling under attack, they have a tendency to retreat. Rather than staying open to new possibilities, they become paralyzed in self-preservation and become dismissive of perspectives from outside groups and different sectors of the community.

School leaders can model open-mindedness and push back against retreat-like behaviors by providing a psychologically safe space, where critical discourse and disagreement is valued. As educators, we all need to continually stretch ourselves. We need to seek out different perspectives that encourage playful and critical debate over new and often uncomfortable ideas.

Seeking out new perspectives and solutions to problems are habits that are essential to learning and adaptation. Leaders can model these habits by expanding their own personal networks and developing relationships with people outside the field of education who can challenge status quo practices and offer different perspectives and insights.

In my first couple of years as superintendent, I was fortunate to form trusting relationships with two business people who had extensive experience in managing large for-profit organizations. Even though their organizations were profit-driven, and the conversations from my end were often uncomfortable (and sometimes defensive), they offered tremendous insights around problem-solving and managing complexity. Their perspectives and insights often differed greatly from my executive team of educators, but were incredibly helpful in stretching me to think about challenges in new and different ways.

This is how I understand the value of the "edge effect" to leadership. According to Vedantam, "the edge is the point in which two ecosystems meet, like the forest and the savannah. And apparently, in ecology, this edge effect is where the most, new life-forms are created."[13]

This high level of creativity emerges from diversity within our organizations and communities, as well. Leaders need to both model and insist on team diversity and social exploratory behaviors that tap into a wide array of diverse social networks. We can easily become immersed in the language and practices of our own discipline and become confident with our own sense of rightness or truth. To enhance learning and creativity within our organizations, we have to look both inwardly, to ensure a diverse composition of employees, and outwardly, to partner with other outside collaborators to create together new, more creative ways forward.

Our human resource practices can provide significant leverage in ensuring diversity. Sarah contends that we tend to hire people in our own image, because we easily connect with them and they make us feel most comfortable. She argues that "we must resist that temptation and instead, hire people who bring something different, who are smarter than us and will stretch and challenge us, in sometimes uncomfortable ways."[14]

Margaret Heffernan agrees and further asserts in her TED Talk, "Dare to Disagree,"[15] that good disagreement is central to progress. She cites research that shows how great research teams, relationships, and organizations foster conditions that allow people to deeply disagree.

Our challenges are great and we need highly talented people with a wide array of perspectives and life experiences to help envision new opportunities and possibilities. As Ken appropriately summarizes, we need people who will stretch us, say no, and challenge us directly, but privately. We cannot afford to surround ourselves with "clones."[16]

Questions for Further Reflection

1. How do you use inquiry in your leadership work?

2. Fullan says that "leaders learn and lead in equal measure." What does that look like for you?

3. In what ways do you empower others?

4. Who on your team challenges and stretches you?

8

Organizational Justice and Disruption

Only those who dare to fail greatly can ever achieve greatly.
—Robert F. Kennedy

Personal courage and rebelliousness are essential attributes for leaders. They are at the core of learning and transformation. Yet as Heifetz and Linsky assert, there is great danger in "challenging the expectations of the people who give you formal and informal authority."[1]

In considering personal courage and rebelliousness when working in a public organization, one must always be mindful of the greater context of the work within the authorizing environment—the board and the community. The board has the power to set expectations and define what it will accept and reject. These expectations often reflect various sources of power and certain constituencies within the broader community. Knowing one's context and what's worth fighting for is essential for a leader.

In this chapter, we will discuss how these leader attributes play out in our organizations. As one would expect, much of this work focused on enhancing organizational learning is embedded in the intentional cultural work of the organization. We will specifically address organizational justice, the de-stigmatization of failure, the paradox of innovative cultures, and the role of disruption in organizational learning.

Organizational Justice

Our aspirations for a more socially just world begin locally within our organizations. We can courageously advocate for social justice for the students and communities we serve, but to make headway in our efforts, we must ensure that we have also assessed the perceptions of justice among our employees. Fair and ethical behavior is at the heart of our work environments. One's sense of justice has a strong impact on one's behavior and attitudes. Researchers have found that how people perceive the fairness of their work environments can impact their commitment to the organization, job performance, and interactions with colleagues.

All employees, regardless of whether they drive a bus or lead a school, are critical to the greater mission and need to be a focal point of leadership efforts. To this end, it can be helpful to think about our work environments from an organizational justice perspective. Organizational justice typically "refers to individual or collective judgments of fairness or ethical propriety. Investigations of organizational justice tend to take a descriptive approach. As such, an event is treated as fair or unfair to the extent that one believes it to be so."[2]

Typically, organizational justice encompasses three areas of focus: distributive, procedural, and interactional justice. Distributive justice deals with the employees' concerns of the fairness of outcomes they receive; procedural justice is concerned with how employees view the fairness of the process of how outcomes are decided. Interactional justice relates to the interpersonal treatment a person receives.

When people perceive their work environment as fair and just, they are more likely to support the mission. In other words, organizational justice fosters a collective investment in the work. When people are invested and engaged in their work they are more likely to pursue personal growth efforts which enhance organizational capacity. A personal and collective commitment to learning and growth contributes to a culture of organizational learning.

When considering the importance of engaging people in complex, messy, and frustrating work, Margaret Wheatley reminds us that we can learn a lot from social movements.

"A movement is defined by the people willing to stay dedicated to their cause for a long time, those who take risks, work hard, expect defeat and still keep going."[3] Leaders need to ensure a similar high level of investment among employees, for an organization to foster learning, adaptation, and innovation.

Destigmatize Failure

We discussed the importance of confronting our fears as individual leaders. This skill needs to be practiced in our schools and districts, as well. Organizations must be adept at using failure as an impetus for deeper learning. Leaders, therefore, need to model taking responsible risks and learning from failure.

We know that failure can be wounding and uncomfortable, so it makes sense that we may try to hide it, deny it, or make excuses. Unfortunately, in the highly politicized and often unforgiving context of public schooling, recognition of a failed initiative can easily become a political nightmare. Each constituency seeks to find someone to blame. Under these highly vulnerable conditions, it is understandable that leaders are reluctant to become targets or scapegoats.

Unfortunately, when we don't accept and make failure transparent, we don't benefit from the organizational learning that is inspired by seeking to better understand what went wrong. When we reject the existence of mistakes and failures, we deny the organization of the deep and dynamic learning necessary for growth and improvement. It sends the resounding message throughout the organization that failure should be avoided at all costs.

There is compelling research that suggests that how we address failure with our employees has consequences for our organizations. According to research by Pury and Lopez,

> Organizational performance is negatively impacted in two scenarios, when managers fail to explicitly state that mistakes would be forgiven and when employees were punished for making mistakes. In both cases, employees were less likely to experiment with new programs or take risks to innovate. In contrast, employees who worked for managers who explicitly communicated their willingness to work through mistakes, as opposed to punishing

individuals who made them, tend to be more innovative and willing to extend themselves and their best thinking to their work.[4]

The role of the leader is critical. When leaders recognize failure as an important part of the human condition they give permission to others to try things and fail, learn, and try again. In other words, "success consists of going from failure to failure without a loss of enthusiasm."[5]

When leaders are transparent around failure and ensure that struggles are brought into the open so everyone can learn from them, they enable a cultural shift to "destigmatize failure."[6] When we destigmatize failure, we shift our mind-sets and conversations to a more action-oriented focus. Individuals and teams are more likely to try new things and test out their theories of action. Essentially when exploration and experimentation are encouraged, failure is accepted as a natural part of the process of learning, and the perceived risk of not doing something to improve becomes greater than the potential risk of failure from taking-action.

Ed Catmull, author of Creativity, Inc., shares his position on the value of failure, "Mistakes aren't a necessary evil. They aren't evil at all. They are an inevitable consequence of doing something new, and as such, should be seen as something valuable; without them we would have no originality."[7]

The Paradox of Innovative Culture

Developing organizations that are agile, creative, and original recognizes the significance of empowering and strengthening others. These cultures are not necessarily easier to manage, however. The leader still needs to manage empowered employees and infuse counterbalancing forces that communicate high expectations for learning and productivity. In his article "The Hard Truth about Innovative Cultures," Gary Pisano[8] reminds us that leaders need to enforce high expectations for performance. He suggests that the freer and more fun aspects of an innovative culture must be counterbalanced by "less fun" behaviors. He describes the following:

> A tolerance for failure requires an intolerance for incompetence. A willingness to experiment requires rigorous discipline.

A Psychological safety requires comfort with brutal candor. Collaboration must be balanced with individual accountability. And flatness requires strong leadership. Innovative cultures are paradoxical. Unless the tensions created by this paradox are carefully managed, attempts to create an innovative culture will fail.

Disruption

Along with their leaders, organizations must continually learn in order to adapt. It is easy to become complacent and comfortable with the status quo. If leaders want to energize their organizations and spark new learning, they often have to orchestrate disruption.

In doing so, Heifetz and Linsky remind us that, "Changing the status quo generates tension and produces heat, by surfacing hidden conflicts and challenging organizational culture."[9] Leaders need to be prepared to recognize and manage the fallout.

When navigating complexity and leading efforts to challenge the status quo, the leader exists within this awkward, not conforming, space. To make an impact the leader needs to rely on others to occupy that space, as well. Board members may be broadly supportive but, with their own agendas, constituencies, and political pressures, are likely less committed to joining the leader in challenging the status quo. This is especially true as board members change, and the board who initially hired the leader is no longer intact.

The leader may orchestrate disruption, but should never embark on change efforts alone. Fortunately, there are typically many others within the organization who are troubled by practices that are ineffective or unjust and are waiting for the opportunity to act in accordance with their values. It is important for the leader to discover and unleash these energizers, in all areas of the organization, whose voices have been silenced through the norms of conformity. According to Quinn and Thakor, "Every organization has a pool of change agents that usually go untapped, and once enlisted can assist with every step of the cultural change."[10]

Although all of us have a desire to feel like we fit in and conformity may make us feel comfortable, it doesn't let us reap the benefits of greater authenticity.

Gino cites one study by *Cable and Kay* that surveyed 2,700 teachers who had been working for a year and reviewed the performance ratings given by their supervisors. Teachers who said they could express their authentic selves received higher ratings than teachers who did not feel they could do so. Numerous studies, across a variety of sectors, have reported similar findings. The usual ways of thinking and doing—play a critical role in shaping performance over time. But they can also get us stuck, decrease our engagement, and constrain our ability to innovate or to perform at a high level.[11]

An important lesson for leaders is that although conformity among our employees makes our lives as supervisors easier, less contentious, and more comfortable, "nonconformity promotes innovation, improves performance, and can enhance a person's standing more than conformity can."[12]

Therefore, as leaders, we need to ensure that we tap into the energy and diversity of our employees and take notice of those, in particular, who dare to disagree.

Eric speaks to the importance of empowerment. When Eric began his current superintendent position his school district was very different from what it is today. The organization was hierarchical and compliant. Staff and students had little voice in decision-making and conformity was the norm. Today the culture gives voice to students and staff, there is a high degree of engagement and all individuals are empowered to grapple with messiness. The culture today emboldens students to practice democratic skills and fight social injustice. It is this high degree of system change that reflects the rebel spirit.

Encouraging people to speak up and resist conformity (for the sake of compliance) can be loud, messy, confusing, and contentious at times, but it also breathes life into our democratic principles and helps prepare our young people to be responsible citizens.

We create energy, tension and discomfort when we disrupt that which is familiar and comfortable, and replace it with ambiguity and messiness. The tension provides tremendous opportunity, but can also be disarming and frightening, if not managed effectively. Therefore, it is critical that leaders leverage the energy and tension to facilitate meaningful learning and growth. In other words, leaders skillfully push back to move forward.

Questions for Further Reflection

1. In what ways have you assessed organizational justice in your district?

2. How does your organization learn from mistakes and failures?

3. Do you feel a need to disrupt your organization? How do you go about doing that?

4. How do you identify and support change agents in your organization?

9

Urgency and Bold Moves

Moving boldly is not moving impulsively or for the sake of change.
Moving boldly involves breaking barriers that need breaking.
　　　　　　　　—Heidi Hayes Jacobs & Marie Hubley Alcock

There is great urgency in the work of leaders and yet often contradictory messages about what that means. As we discussed in chapter 5, leaders often personally thrive on a sense of adventure and challenge. The driving force, however, behind their restlessness is truly less about their individual attributes and more about their aspirations for the students and communities they serve. In this chapter, we consider enhancing organizational learning and adaptation by cultivating a sense of organizational urgency and employing bold moves. In addressing these organizational growth attributes, we focus on the nature of urgency, the necessity of systemic change, and both the will and courage to act boldly.

Urgency

The leaders I interviewed were neither patient nor apologetic. The idea that leaders take their time, learn the culture, work toward consensus, and so on—in other words, the textbook approach to the first one hundred days—dramatically shifted for these leaders with each new position. After serving in more than one formal leadership position, their patience for change was gone. They all reported feeling a much greater sense of urgency.

Eric stated, "We need to do what needs to be done and do it with urgency . . . we need to abandon wait time."[1] In essence, the common consensus among experienced leaders was that the students have one opportunity to experience school and there is no time to waste.

Kelley shared a similar perspective, as she gained experience she came to the strong realization that she was "no longer interested in running around the hamster wheel. Leaders need to recognize that they have limited time, and need to be always moving forward."[2]

Moving with a sense of urgency, while better ensuring one's ability to be effective, is also a matter of timing. Kelley shared that the first year in a position is a critical time for a leader, because it is the only time one can truly view the organization through fresh eyes.

> You are not a part of the culture yet, so you can still look at things through a more neutral lens—once you become more integrated this is very difficult to do. It is also when the leader has the highest degree of confidence, because typically the Board members who hired the leader are deeply invested and committed to making it work. With each board election these dynamics can change dramatically.[3]

Max shared that when you have a good team you can develop and nurture a sense of urgency. He was also mindful of the pace of change and the importance of not moving too quickly—"never get out over your skis."[4]

One's sense of urgency as a leader is also related to how one understands the nature of the work. Heifetz and Linsky share from their research that the most common source of leadership failure is that leaders "treat adaptive challenges like technical problems."[5]

How the challenge is framed and defined is crucial. *Technical change* requires changes in routine behaviors and preferences; uses existing knowledge and skills; is directed from above; and deploys existing competence in a different context. *Adaptive change*, on the other hand, requires new ways of thinking about the organization's work; needs changes in knowledge, skills, and dispositions; is internalized and implemented by stakeholders; and recognizes that existing competence may no longer be relevant or adequate.[6]

Defining the nature of the problem or challenge accurately is an essential part of the leader's work. A leader can spend considerable time and resources tinkering with a poorly defined problem, rather than building capacity through adaptive and systemic work.

The leaders I interviewed shared, that over time they grew to more fully appreciate the complexity and intensity of the work and became better at defining the adaptive nature of the challenges they faced. Marsha stated, "With experience, I knew the length of time that it would take when dealing with larger systems; whereas when you first start out, you don't really know the amount of heavy lifting that is in front of you for the change to be effective."[7]

At the same time, leaders recognize that along with a sense of urgency, timing, and an appreciation for the complexity of the work, there is also the personal investment. Once you commit to do something, you invest fully. Leadership matters. Max shared that he learned early on that as a leader you have to be "all in" like "the polar plunge—If you are going to commit you have to do it all the way."[8]

Systems Change

Experienced leaders can often describe several initiatives that they were successful in implementing, but are quick to acknowledge that although these efforts may have improved conditions there is still so much that needs to be done. In one district, I felt some satisfaction when we finally, after extensive work, developed and implemented a two-way language immersion program and an alternative high school. Although these initiatives addressed some immediate and pressing issues, they did little to profoundly impact the larger system or nature of schooling itself.

My experiences were not unusual. Leaders engage in a lot of good work, but also recognize that much of it is tinkering. Even when the goals are broad, actions explicit and the outcomes evident, the lasting, sustainable nature of change efforts are often fragile. The status quo is incredibly powerful. As board members change, and leaders move on, the organization struggles to maintain a sense of equilibrium. New leaders may have their own agendas, and if there are not enough powerful change forces in play to support the progress, the status quo is likely to reassert itself.

Sarah describes how in one district she worked diligently to increase the diversity of her staff and to implement a more globally focused curriculum. When she left the school district those aspirational initiatives were no longer a priority, and quickly fell out of favor. She reflected, "there are some incredible opportunities to be successful, but you are equally likely to not reach your goals."[9]

Leaders expend a tremendous amount of energy, effort, and political and social capital attempting to lead meaningful and significant change. In doing so, they realize that there are personal and professional risks, as well as a wide array of potentially heart-wrenching compromises. Leaders over time learn the necessity of having measured expectations.

Learning from many false starts, our leaders shared that over time they grew to more fully appreciate the need to resist pressure to embrace the latest program or fad, to be informed but not driven by data, and to challenge fragmented approaches to reform. The education literature is full of recipes for improvement, but the reality is there are no prescriptions or quick fixes in adaptive work.

Eric described that in his earlier days as a leader, he gravitated to all the latest programs and initiatives, now he understands the importance of investing deeply in systems change. He shared his challenge to "de-track" his high school curriculum and structure, in order to serve all students well. "This systemic initiative disrupted a culture of structured elitism where students in the same school had widely varied opportunities and experiences, based on which curriculum track they were assigned. This extremely challenging effort has impacted all aspects of schooling."[10] It has also paved the way to a more open culture where continuous learning and experimentation is embraced.

The practices that most deeply impact the system are generally the most challenging to change. When we talk about bold moves we recognize that the system is complex and made up of many parts and the connections and relationships matter. A system that is constantly learning and improving is mindful of the context, conditions, and connections, as well as the fluid nature of leading change.

As Fullan and Quinn describe, we are working with a new change dynamic today that "shifts from the notion of sequential, discrete stages of traditional alignment to a more organic process of diffusion and continuous learning."[11]

Bold Moves

System change requires bold and continuous movement that makes sense within one's context. Bold moves are necessary, but we cannot assume that all "best practices" are transferable. Leaders need to understand their context well and move with a disciplined focus in leading change. "Failure to fully appreciate the significance of context has often led good reform efforts to fail."[12] The roles, relationships, and structures of schooling are all contextual. Challenging our assumptions about these potential inhibitors, within our own context, is central to our improvement efforts.

Bold moves are ultimately a result of difficult choices. When we adapt to new conditions we decide what is essential to preserve going forward and what can be left behind.

For organizations to adapt quickly, leaders need to habitually and collectively grapple with essential questions that foster a thoughtful, future-focused discourse.

Ethnographer and author Simon Sinek suggests that our questions should initially begin with "why?" "When most organizations or people think, act or communicate they do so from the outside in, from WHAT to WHY. And for good reason—they go from clearest thing to the fuzziest thing. We say WHAT we do, we sometimes say HOW we do it, but we rarely say WHY we do WHAT we do."[13]

It is important for educators to begin with why, as well—for example, why do we exist? Or why do we do what we do? Grounded in a shared sense of purpose, we can then better engage in adaptive discourse around:

- What from the past do we need to let go?
- What should we continue?
- What do we need to create?
- How does what we do impact our system and who benefits? (equity, efficiency, and effectiveness)

The practice of establishing organizational habits and protocols for questioning, challenging assumptions, and taking action enables greater organizational adaptation and agility. When leaders routinely model and practice higher level questioning and iterative, designed-based improvement efforts, members of the organization become better equipped to address adaptive challenges.

As we discussed in the previous chapter, when attempting bold moves and stimulating deep changes within the organization, the leader is also raising tension and discomfort. It is important, therefore that,

> The leader controls the temperature. There are really two tasks here. The first is to raise the heat enough so that people sit up, pay attention, and deal with the real threats facing them. Without some stress there is no incentive for them to change anything. The second is to lower the tension when necessary to reduce a counter-productive level of tension. Any community can take only so much pressure before it becomes either immobilized or spins out of control.[14]

Bold moves can have a big impact, but they can also fail. Adaptive leadership adjusts to both the successes and failures—it is delicate and nuanced. As Sarah states, "over time you learn the roadmap and become more skilled at adapting—It is important to have measured expectations and enough resilience to stay the course. The real joy is to be able to cultivate something that makes a difference and lasts."[15]

Questions for Further Reflection

1. In what ways do you experience a sense of urgency?

2. What does systems work mean to you? What challenges are associated with addressing the "system"?

3. When considering your current work, how do you distinguish between technical problems and adaptive challenges?

4. What "bold moves" are you engaged in?

10

Leading to Learn

Executives today face two competing demands. They must execute in order to meet today's challenges. And they must adapt what and how things get done in order to thrive in tomorrow's world. They must develop "next practices" while excelling at today's best practices.
—Ronald Heifetz & Marty Linsky

Leadership is a work in progress. We constantly strive but never arrive. Each journey is characterized by incredible challenges and unlimited opportunities to learn. There is no one right path to follow and often the road most traveled is thwart with obstacles along the way. Our personal identity is often tenuous, as we constantly grapple with our need for both preservation and reinvention. We share our stories while concurrently re-writing them.

In a world of messiness and fast-paced change, the one constant is our ability to learn. As leaders who strive to make a lasting impact, it is essential that we continue to build our capacity for personal and organizational learning.

A critical assumption addressed throughout the book, however, is that personal learning is not a given. It is uncomfortable and at times frightening. It often shakes our confidence and sense of identity. When we truly engage as a learner we become vulnerable to new discoveries about ourselves and our organizations. Shifting from operating in a knowing mode to a learning one is deeply challenging. Prioritizing learning over knowing requires more than surface-level actions, particularly in highly visible executive positions.

Leaders are expected to exude confidence and articulate a strong knowledge base. This expectation on the part of others profoundly shapes what we expect from ourselves. When entrusted in a position of power it is easy to overestimate our personal expertise and relevancy. Our identities are fragile, particularly when we perceive them as fixed, and sometimes, our egos and "need to be needed" get in the way. There is great pressure to know and play the role of "expert," and as long as we don't go too deep in our inquiries, our problem-solving may seem legitimate, and in some cases sufficient. In leadership positions, where concerns about legitimacy and credibility are paramount, there are tremendous risks to becoming vulnerable to new truths.

There are also many distractions and obstacles that make it difficult to fully embrace learning. The pace and context of leadership are not conducive to slower more deliberate thinking and analysis. Deep learning requires processing time, and this is incongruent with the "quick fix it" demands and expectations of a context that is fast-moving and generally unforgiving. Leaders also become adept at making excuses and defending their sense of rightness. Survival becomes a priority over learning.

Leaders engage in many forms of professional development, but unfortunately, so much of the focus is on absorbing content and does not fundamentally contribute to deeper learning or behavioral change. Simply being committed to learning is not enough. Leaders need to further develop their capacity for learning.

Throughout the book, we addressed eight attributes that when further developed make leaders more receptive to deep learning. Although the list is certainly not exhaustive, each attribute is associated with research that supports how further development can contribute to effective leadership during rapidly changing times. The attributes include *aspiration and agility; curiosity and intellectual humility; courage and rebelliousness; and enthusiasm and a driving spirit.* Collectively, these attributes focus a leader's work on learning, adaptation, and innovation.

It is not sufficient, however, for leaders to develop their personal capacity for learning. In our new learning economy, they also need to lead their organizations in learning. Developing and nurturing the capacity for both personal and organizational learning is highly nuanced.

Organizations need to be equipped with the attributes and conditions for deep learning for individuals to learn and contribute to organizational learning. This means that leaders may need to rebel or disrupt status quo practices in order to develop and sustain fertile conditions for learning within the organization. In other words, as leaders are continually developing the personal attributes and competencies to lead organizational learning, they are also transforming their organizations from operating in a knowing to a learning mode. They are building the capacity for organizational learning and agility by strengthening the organizational attributes of *purpose, imagination, exploration, diversity, organizational justice, disruption, bold moves, and a high degree of urgency.* Essentially, they are situating themselves and their organizations to thrive and make an impact in a world of discomfort, ambiguity, and messiness.

Questions for Further Reflection

1. What do you personally want to learn?
2. How will you make learning central to your leadership?
3. What do you want your organization to learn?
4. How will you make learning central to your organization?

Conclusion

With learning at the heart of our work as leaders, I want to thank my exceptional colleagues who openly shared their personal learning. Each of them embraces a passion for learning and exploration. They epitomize the belief that "leadership is an experimental art and life is a leadership laboratory."[1]

When we approach life and leadership as opportunities to learn, we continually evolve as leaders. Through continuous trial and error, we build our capacity to lead socially just and meaningful change. We are humbled by the responsibility, and truly grateful for the journey.

Notes

Introduction

1. Bradley Staats, *Never Stop Learning, Stay Relevant, Reinvent Yourself, and Thrive* (Boston, MA: Harvard Business Review Press, 2018), 4.
2. Ronald A. Heifetz, Alexander Grashow, and Marty Linsky, *The Practice of Adaptive Leadership: Tools and Tactics for Changing your Organization and the World* (Boston, MA: Harvard Business Review Press, 2009), XX.

Chapter 1

1. Margaret J. Wheatley, *Who Do We Choose to Be? Facing Reality, Claiming Leadership, Restoring Sanity* (Oakland, CA: Berrett-Koehler Publishers, 2017), p. 13.
2. Staats, *Never Stop Learning*, p. 4.
3. Ibid.
4. Ibid., 7–8.
5. Tom Chi, "Knowing Is the Enemy of Learning," TED Talk, February 6, 2014.
6. Ibid.
7. Ibid.
8. Heather McGowan, "The Paradox of Education: Learning Over Knowing," *Core Education*, January 20, 2016. http://www.coreeducationllc.com/blog2/the-paradox-of-education-learning-over-knowing/.
9. Ibid.
10. National Academies of Sciences, Engineering and Medicine et al., *How People Learn II: Learners, Contexts and Cultures* (Washington, DC: The National Academies Press, 2018), p. 201.
11. Ibid., 223.
12. Daniel Kahneman, *Thinking Fast and Slow* (New York, NY: Farrar, Straus and Giroux, 2011), 21–24.

Chapter 2

1. Emily Esfahani Smith, "The Two Stories We Tell Ourselves," TED Ideas, January 12, 2017.
2. Ibid., 2017.
3. David Behlow, interview by Mary Herrmann, September 19, 2018, Illinois.
4. Marsha Chappelow, interview by Mary Herrmann, October 21, 2018, Kansas.
5. Herminia Ibarra, "The Authenticity Paradox," *Harvard Business Review* 93 (2015): 54–59.
6. Jennifer Cheatham, interview by Mary Herrmann, November 16, 2018, Wisconsin.
7. Cory Collins, "What Is White Privilege, Anyway?" *Teaching Tolerance*, Fall 2018.
8. Dolly Chugh, "How to Let Go of Being a Good Person and Become a Better One," TED@BCG, October 2018.
9. Sarah Jerome, interview by Mary Herrmann, December 2018, Wisconsin.
10. Herminia Ibarra, *Act Like a Leader, Think Like a Leader* (Boston, MA: Harvard Business Review Press, 2015), pp. 121–123.
11. Ibid., 122.
12. Jerome, 2018.
13. Susan David, "The Gift and Power of Emotional Courage," TED Talk, November 2017.
14. Monique Valcour and John McNulty, "To Make a Change at Work, Tell Yourself a Different Story," *Harvard Business Review*, August 24, 2018.
15. Behlow, 2018.
16. Ken Arndt, interview by Mary Herrmann, October 5, 2018, Illinois.
17. Cheatham, 2018.
18. Behlow, 2018.

Chapter 3

1. Staats, *Never Stop Learning*, 63.
2. Ronald Heifetz and Marty Linsky, *Leadership on the Line: Staying Alive Through the Dangers of Leading* (Boston, MA: Harvard Business School Press, 2017), p. 14.
3. Staats, *Never Stop Learning*, 63.

4. Julie Galef, "Why You Think You're Right Even When You're Wrong," TED Talk, February 2016. https://www.ted.com/talks/julia_galef_why_you_think_you_re_right_even_if_you_re_wrong?language=en.
5. Galef, "Why You Think," 2016.
6. Ibid.
7. Shankar Vedantam and Francesca Gino, "You 2.0: Rebel with a Cause," *Hidden Brain*, July 23, 2018. https://www.npr.org/2018/07/23/631524581/you-2-0-rebel-with-a-cause.
8. Vedantam and Gino, "You 2.0: Rebel with a Cause," 2018.
9. Kelley Kalinich, interviewed by Mary Herrmann on Oct. 24, 2018. Illinois.
10. Cheatham, 2018.
11. Michael Fullan, *Nuance: Why Some Leaders Succeed and Others Fail* (Thousand Oaks, CA: Corwin, 2019), 12.
12. Behlow, 2018.
13. Arndt, 2018.

Chapter 4

1. Brené Brown, *Dare to Lead: Brave Work, Tough Conversations, Whole Hearts* (New York, NY: Random House, 2018), 24.
2. Cheatham, 2018.
3. Behlow, 2018.
4. Matt Brubaker and Foster Mobley, "Don't Let Your Inner Fears Destroy Your Careers," *Harvard Business Review*, October 17, 2017.
5. Staats, *Never Stop Learning*, 21.
6. Bear Grylls, "Adventurer Bear Grylls Shares His Tips on How to Stay Alive," *On Point*, October 2, 2018. https://www.wbur.org/onpoint/2018/10/02/bear-grylls-how-to-stay-alive.
7. Cathy Lassiter, *Everyday Courage for School Leaders* (Thousand Oaks, CA: Corwin, 2018), 12.
8. Lassiter, *Everyday Courage*, 13.
9. Francesca Gino, "Rebel with a Cause," *Hidden Brain*, July 23, 2018. https://www.npr.org/2018/07/23/631524581/you-2-0-rebel-with-a-cause.
10. Eric Witherspoon, interview by Mary Herrmann, November 1, 2018, Illinois.
11. Gino, "Rebel with a Cause," 2018.
12. Arndt, 2018.
13. Cheatham, 2018.
14. Kalinich, 2018.

Chapter 5

1. Witherspoon, 2018.
2. Behlow, 2018.
3. Cheatham, 2018.
4. Max McGee, interview by Mary Herrmann, January 8, 2019, Illinois.
5. Joseph Folkman, "New Research: 7 Ways to Become a More Resilient Leader," *Forbes*, April 6, 2017.
6. Jesse Sostrin, "Strategy + Business Blog," May 22, 2018. https://www.strategy-business.com/author?author=Jesse+Sostrin
7. Jerome, 2018.
8. Keith Marty, interview by Mary Herrmann, November 21, 2018, Missouri.
9. Marc Effron, *8 Steps to High Performance: Focus on What You Can Change, Ignore the Rest* (Boston, MA: Harvard Business Review Press, 2018), 50.

Chapter 6

1. McGee, 2019.
2. Chimamanda Adichie, "The Danger of a Single Story," TED Talk, July 2009. https://www.ted.com/talks/chimamanda_adichie_the_danger_of_a_single_story?language=en.
3. Fullan, *Nuance*, 18.
4. Wheatley, *Who Do We Choose to Be?*, 109.
5. Ibid., 168.
6. Stephen Dubner, "Can an Industrial Giant Become a Tech Darling?" *Freakonomics Radio*, November 7, 2018. http://freakonomics.com/podcast/ford/.
7. Fullan, *Nuance*, 10.
8. Jerome, 2018.
9. Marty, 2018.

Chapter 7

1. Behlow, 2018.
2. Arndt, 2018.
3. David L. Cooperrider and Diana Whitney, *A Positive Revolution in Change: Appreciative Inquiry* (Taos, NM: Corporation for Positive Change, 1999), XX. https://appreciativeinquiry.champlain.edu/learn/appreciative-inquiry-introduction/5-classic-principles-ai/.

4. Ibid., XX.
5. Beth Comstock, *Imagine It Forward: Courage, Creativity and the Power of Change* (New York, NY: Crown Publishing, 2018), p. 130.
6. National Academies of Sciences et al., *How People Learn II*, 197.
7. Stephanie Hirsh, 4 *Cornerstones of Professional Learning: Fundamental Principles Pave the Way for Educators' Actions* (Oxford, OH: Learning Forward, 2019), pp. 1–11.
8. Fullan, *Nuance*, 16.
9. Jesse Sostrin, "To Be a Great Leader You Have to Learn to Delegate Well," *Harvard Business Review*, October 10, 2017.
10. Kathryn Boudett and Elizabeth City, *Meeting Wise: Making the Most of Collaborative Time for Educators* (Cambridge, MA: Harvard Education Press, 2014), 11.
11. Fullan, *Nuance*, 72.
12. Shankar Vedantam, "The Edge Effect," *Hidden Brain*, July 2, 2018. https://www.npr.org/2018/07/02/625426015/the-edge-effect.
13. Ibid.
14. Jerome, 2018.
15. Margaret Heffernan, "Dare to Disagree," TED Talk, June 2012. https://www.ted.com/talks/margaret_heffernan_dare_to_disagree? language=en.
16. Arndt, 2018.

Chapter 8

1. Heifetz and Linsky, *Leadership on the Line*, 27.
2. Psychology Research and Reference, "Organizational Justice," *Psychology*, accessed January 2011. https://psychology.iresearch net.com/industrial-organizational-psychology/job-satisfaction/organizational-justice/.
3. Wheatley, *Who Do We Choose to Be?* 158.
4. Cynthia L. S. Pury and Shane J. Lopez, eds., *The Psychology of Courage: Modern Research on an Ancient Virtue* (Washington, DC: American Psychological Association, 2010), 9–22; 247.
5. Staats, *Never Stop Learning*, 36.
6. Ibid., 32.
7. Ibid., 34.
8. Gary Pisano, "The Hard Truth about Innovative Cultures," *Harvard Business Review*, 62–71, January–February 2019.
9. Heifetz and Linsky, *Leadership on the Line*, 107–108.

10. Robert Quinn and Anjan Thakor, "Creating a Purpose-Driven Organization," *Harvard Business Review*, July–August 2018.
11. Francesca Gino, "Rebel Talent," *HBR.ORG, THE BIG IDEA*, October–November 2016, https://www.hbs.edu/faculty/Publication%20Files/Let%20your%20workers%20rebel_b87d0da9-de68-45be-a026-22dee862e6e4.pdf.
12. Gino, "Rebel Talent," 2016.

Chapter 9

1. Witherspoon, 2018.
2. Kalinich, 2018.
3. Ibid.
4. McGee, 2019.
5. Heifetz and Linsky, *Leadership on the Line*, 2002.
6. Ibid., 13–20.
7. Chappelow, 2018.
8. McGee, 2019.
9. Jerome, 2018.
10. Witherspoon, 2018.
11. Fullan, M and Joanne Quinn. *Coherence: The Right Drivers in Action for Schools, Districts and Systems*. Thousand Oaks: Corwin, 2015.
12. Bryk, A., Gomez, L., Grunow, A. and Paul LeMahieu, *Learning to Improve: How America's Schools Can Get Better at Getting Better*, Cambridge, MA: Harvard Education Press 2015.
13. Simon Sinek, "How Great Leaders Inspire Action," TED Talk, September 2009. https://www.ted.com/talks/simon_sinek_how_great_leaders_inspire_action?language=en.
14. Heifetz and Linsky, *Leadership on the Line*, 108.
15. Jerome, 2018.

Conclusion

1. Heifetz, Grashow, and Linsky, *The Practice of Adaptive Leadership*, 44.

References

Adichie, Chimamanda. "The Danger of a Single Story." Filmed July 2009 at TED Global. https://www.ted.com/talks/chimamanda_adichie_the_danger_of_a_single_story?language=en.

Boudett, Kathryn and Elizabeth City. *Meeting Wise: Making the Most of Collaborative Time for Educators.* Cambridge, MA: Harvard Education Press, 2014.

Brown, Brené. *Dare to Lead: Brave Work, Tough Conversations, Whole Hearts.* New York, NY: Random House, 2018.

Brubaker, Matt and Foster Mobley. "Don't Let Your Inner Fears Destroy Your Careers." *Harvard Business Review*, October 17, 2017.

Bryk, A., Gomez, L., Grunow, A. and Paul LeMahieu, *Learning to Improve: How America's Schools Can Get Better at Getting Better*, Cambridge, MA: Harvard Education Press 2015.

Chi, Tom. "Knowing Is the Enemy of Learning." Filmed February 6, 2014, at TEDxSemesteratSea. https://www.youtube.com/watch?v=_WtsMrkfG1w.

Chugh, Dolly. "How to Let Go of Being a Good Person and Become a Better One." Filmed October 2018 at TED@BCG. https://www.ted.com/talks/dolly_chugh_how_to_let_go_of_being_a_good_person_and_become_a_better_person?language=en.

Collins, Cory. "What Is White Privilege, Anyway?" *Teaching Tolerance*, Fall 2018.

Comstock, Beth. *Imagine It Forward: Courage, Creativity and the Power of Change.* New York, NY: Crown Publishing, 2018.

Cooperrider, David L. and Diana Whitney. *A Positive Revolution in Change: Appreciative Inquiry.* Taos, NM: Corporation for Positive Change, 1999. https://appreciativeinquiry.champlain.edu/learn/appreciative-inquiry-introduction/5-classic-principles-ai/.

David, Susan. "The Gift and Power of Emotional Courage." Filmed November 2017 at TEDWomen. https://www.ted.com/talks/susan_david_the_gift_and_power_of_emotional_courage?language=en.

Dubner, Stephen. "Can an Industrial Giant Become a Tech Darling?" *Freakonomics Radio*, November 7, 2018. http://freakonomics.com/podcast/ford/.

Effron, Marc. *8 Steps to High Performance: Focus on What You Can Change, Ignore the Rest.* Boston, MA: Harvard Business Review Press, 2018.

Esfahani Smith, Emily. "The Two Kinds of Stories We Tell about Ourselves." *Ideas.TED.com*, January 12, 2017. https://ideas.ted.com/the-two-kinds-of-stories-we-tell-about-ourselves/.

Folkman, Joseph. "New Research: 7 Ways to Become a More Resilient Leader." *Forbes*, April 6, 2017.

Fullan, Michael. *Nuance: Why Some Leaders Succeed and Others Fail.* Thousand Oaks, CA: Corwin, 2019.

Fullan, M and Joanne Quinn. *Coherence: The Right Drivers in Action for Schools, Districts and Systems.* Thousand Oaks: Corwin, 2015.

Galef, Julie. "Why You Think You're Right Even When You're Wrong." Filmed February 2016 at TED. https://www.ted.com/talks/julia_galef.

Gino, Francesca. "Rebel Talent." *HBR.ORG, THE BIG IDEA*, October–November 2016. https://www.hbs.edu/faculty/Publication%20Files/Let%20your%20workers%20rebel_b87d0da9-de68-45be-a026-22dee862e6e4.pdf.

Gino, Francesca. "Rebel with a Cause." *Hidden Brain Podcast*, July 23, 2018. https://www.npr.org/2018/07/23/631524581/you-2-0-rebel-with-a-cause.

Grylls, Bear. "Adventurer Bear Grylls Shares His Tips on How to Stay Alive." *On Point, NPR*, October 2, 2018. https://www.wbur.org/onpoint/2018/10/02/bear-grylls-how-to-stay-alive.

Heffernan, Margaret. "Dare to Disagree." Filmed June 2012 at TED Talk. https://www.ted.com/talks/margaret_heffernan_dare_to_disagree?language=en.

Heifetz, Ronald A., Alexander Grashow, and Marty Linsky. *The Practice of Adaptive Leadership: Tools and Tactics for Changing your Organization and the World.* Boston, MA: Harvard Business Press, 2009.

Heifetz, Ronald A., and Marty Linsky. *Leadership on the Line: Staying Alive through the Dangers of Leading.* Boston, MA: Harvard Business Press, 2017.

Herrmann, Mary B. *Decide to Lead: Building Capacity and Leveraging Change through Decision-Making.* Lanham, MD: Rowman & Littlefield, 2017.

Hirsh, Stephanie. *4 Cornerstones of Professional Learning: Fundamental Principles Pave the Way for Educators' Actions.* Oxford, OH: Learning Forward, 2019.

Ibarra, Herminia. *Act Like a Leader, Think Like a Leader*. Boston, MA: Harvard Business Review Press, 2015.

Ibarra, Herminia. "The Authenticity Paradox." *Harvard Business Review* 93, no. 1/2 (2015): 54–59.

Kahneman, Daniel. *Thinking Fast and Slow*. New York, NY: Farrar, Straus and Giroux, 2011.

Lassiter, Cathy. *Everyday Courage for School Leaders*. Thousand Oaks, CA: Corwin, 2018.

McGowan, Heather. "The Paradox of Education: Learning over Knowing." *Core Education*, January 20, 2016.

National Academies of Sciences, Engineering and Medicine, et al. *How People Learn II*. Washington, DC: National Academies Press, 2018.

Pisano, Gary. "The Hard Truth about Innovative Cultures." *Harvard Business Review*, January–February 2019.

Psychology. "Organizational Justice." *Psychology*, accessed January 2011. https://psychology.iresearchnet.com/industrial-organizational-psychology/job-satisfaction/organizational-justice/.

Pury, Cynthia L. S. and Shane J. Lopez, eds., *The Psychology of Courage: Modern Research on an Ancient Virtue*. Washington, DC: American Psychological Association, 2010.

Quinn, Robert E. and Anjan V. Thakor. "Creating a Purpose-Driven Organization." *Harvard Business Review*, July–August 2018.

Sinek, Simon. "How Great Leaders Inspire Action." Filmed September 2009 at TED. https://www.ted.com/talks/simon_sinek_how_great_leaders_inspire_action?language=en.

Sostrin, Jesse. "Strategy + Business Blog." May 22, 2018. https://www.strategy-business.com/author?author=Jesse+Sostrin

Sostrin, Jesse. "To Be a Great Leader You Have to Learn to Delegate Well." *Harvard Business Review*, October 10, 2017.

Staats, Bradley R. *Never Stop Learning, Stay Relevant, Reinvent Yourself, and Thrive*. Boston, MA: Harvard Business Review Press, 2018.

Valcour, Monique, and John McNulty. "To Make a Change at Work, Tell Yourself a Different Story." *Harvard Business Review*, August 24, 2018.

Vedantam, Shankar. "The Edge Effect." *Hidden Brain*, July 2, 2018. https://www.npr.org/2018/07/02/625426015/the-edge-effect.

Vedantam, Shankar and Francesca Gino. "You 2.0: Rebel with a Cause." *Hidden Brain*, July 23, 2018.

Wheatley, Margaret J. *Who Do We Choose To Be? Facing Reality, Claiming Leadership, Restoring Sanity*. Oakland, CA: Berrett-Koehler Publishers, 2017.

Index

www.ingramcontent.com/pod-product-compliance
Lightning Source LLC
Chambersburg PA
CBHW050219270326
41914CB00003BA/478